HAWKER

HAWKER

Aviator, Designer, Test Pilot

by

L . K . B L A C K M O R E

Orion Books / New York

Published in the United States in 1991 by Orion Books, a division of Crown Publishers, Inc., 201 East 50th Street, New York, New York 10022. Member of the Crown Publishing Group.

Originally published in 1990 in New Zealand by David Bateman, Ltd.

ORION and colophon are trademarks of Crown Publishers, Inc.

Manufactured in the United States of America

Library of Congress Cataloging-in-Publication Data

Blackmore, L. K.
    Hawker : a biography of Harry Hawker / by L.K. Blackmore ; foreword by Sir Thomas Sopwith.
        p.   cm.
    Includes index.
    1. Hawker, H. G. (Harry George) 1889–1921.   2. Aeronautics—Great Britain—Biography.   I. Title.
TL540.H3B53   1991
629.13′0092—dc20   90-22699
[B]   CIP

    ISBN 0-517-57777-1

10 9 8 7 6 5 4 3 2 1

First American Edition

Dedication

Hawker was one of the very early aviators who possessed the ability to design, engineer and pilot an aircraft; he coupled this with exceptional courage.

This book is dedicated to his memory and the memories of other pioneer aviators.

Acknowledgements

There are many people who have helped with this biography. I would particularly like to thank the following Hawker Siddeley Australia companies — Hawker Pacific Pty Ltd, Hawker de Havilland Ltd and Hawker Noyes Pty Ltd, for their support in sponsoring the publication of this book. Also Chris Ryland, Managing Director of Hawker Pacific for the Epilogue and Company Secretary Ian Greaves for all his help.

It is not possible to name everyone but my special thanks go to: Bob Chamberlain, nephew of Harry Hawker, for all his photographic and archival material; John Crampton; Michael White of David Bateman Ltd, my tireless publisher, and his assistants, Derrin Osborn and Mary Harris; Ian Kirkpatrick; Bruce Robertson; Peter Dawson, Curator of the Museum at St Johns, Newfoundland; Barbara Wheeler; Ann Wardrop; Capt Mike Russell; and Charles Schaedel.

I am also grateful for Sir Thomas Sopwith's kindness in writing the Foreword shortly before his death at the age of 101.

Finally I would like to sincerely thank my wife Patricia, who supported me with unstinting enthusiasm and encouragement, and whose knowledge of the family helped so much.

Photographs from known sources are acknowledged below. In some cases, though I have made every effort, I have been unable to establish the source but many of these I believe to be in the public domain as they are well over 50 years old.

Australia Post, 69; Australian War Memorial, 119, 121-123, 132, 133; L.K. Blackmore, 31 (upper); British Aerospace, 226; J.M. Bruce/G.S. Leslie, 128 (2), 129 (2), 218 (upper); Bob Chamberlain, 10, 28-30, 31 (lower), 34 (2), 37, 41, 44 (2), 45, 48, 58, 62, 72 (2), 76 (2), 77, 78, 82, 84, 90 (2), 91, 93, 96, 97, 100, 105, 109, 111, 186 (lower); John Crampton, 52, 53, 114, 186 (upper), 201; Daily Mail, 69; Bert Hawker, 46; H.G. Hawker/K. Mackenzie Grieve, 152 (2), 153; Muriel Hawker, 17, 19, 63, 139, 142, 145 (2), 156 (2), 168 (upper), 187, 196, 199, 207; National Library of Australia, 26, 68, 75, 159, 162, 163, 166, 167 (2), 170 (lower), 206, 209; Quadrant, 204; RAF, 221; Bruce Robertson, 55, 170 (upper), 188, 194, 218 (lower); Sphere Newspaper, 24, 172; St Johns Museum, 14, 20, 21, 150, 155 (2), 168 (lower), 169, 173; The Bulletin of the Vintage Sports Car Club, 182; The Times, 165, 175-181.

Contents

HAWKER

Foreword

I well remember Harry Hawker joining our small company as a mechanic at Brooklands in 1912. He was a glutton for work and was a thoroughly practical fellow in every way. We were running a flying school at the time and one day he asked me if I would teach him to fly. In answer to the question, "What happens if you break the aeroplane?" he took, from inside his sock, fifty pounds — perhaps his entire life savings — and asked if that would do.

After a few lessons he became master of the art. Not only was he a natural pilot but he had a very good eye for the design of aeroplanes and I give him most of the credit for the success of the aeroplanes we went on to make.

He was a quiet fellow, not given to suffering fools gladly, a bit like Sydney Camm who came later.

Mr Blackmore, in co-operation with Hawker's relations in Australia, has thoroughly researched the life of this man who made such an outstanding contribution to the early days of aviation.

Sir Thomas Sopwith CBE

Author's note: The reason the foreword is not signed is that Sir Thomas was 99 years of age and almost totally blind at the time he dictated it to his agent, Lt Col D.G. St J. Radcliffe. Sir Thomas died in 1989 at the age of 101.

Harry George Hawker, MBE, AFC.

Introduction

A most unusual set of circumstances, which I relate below, prompted me to write this book.

Back in 1928 two little girls, Patricia and Joan Keogh, aged four and two, whose mother had died in a diphtheria epidemic, were taken in by the Chamberlain family who lived in a suburb of Melbourne, Australia. Mrs Chamberlain, Maude, was an elder sister of Harry Hawker and was obviously a very compassionate woman. She had two sons, Alan Hawker Chamberlain (Bob) aged 20, and Howard Francis Chamberlain (Bill) then 18. These two little girls grew up in the Chamberlain household. The elder one, Patricia, in the course of time married the author.

Reminiscences of her early life with the Chamberlains, which remain evergreen, reveal that she had been a part of a very vital family which had obviously inherited a good measure of the Hawker genius and a penchant for constructive, hard work. Both Bob and Bill grew up to be distinguished engineers in their own right, culminating in the design and manufacture of the well known Chamberlain tractor and associated farming equipment.

Pat has a vivid memory of a family home filled with memorabilia, photographs and newspaper clippings of Harry and his exploits. He was frequently the subject of conversation and was held almost in reverence by the family. Unfortunately most of this information, including newspaper cuttings and flying journals relating to Harry's work, was lost just after the death of Mrs Chamberlain. Luckily a little of this material was salvaged and remains in the possession of Bob Chamberlain, together with a book written by Harry's wife Muriel the year after he was tragically killed in a flying accident. There is also a book written by Harry himself on the Atlantic attempt.

These stories stimulated my interest and as time went by I became close friends with both Bob and Bill who expressed an interest in having the material published in a biography of Hawker. My involvement has no doubt been accentuated by my lifelong interest in aeroplanes and my early flying training in the venerable Tiger Moth.

This book would not have been possible but for the help and encouragement of Bob Chamberlain who has loaned me the documents and photographs he has held over the years. As well he set down his recollections of events which had not previously been recorded.

Quite separately, and fortuitously, I had become friendly with John Crampton DFC, AFC and Bar, MRAeS, who had been with the Hawker Siddeley Company. When I mentioned my idea of a biography it transpired that he had delivered a paper to the Royal Aeronautical Society on the *Life and Work of H.G. Hawker AFC* in 1979, and another to the Institution of Mechanical Engineers in 1968 entitled *From Sopwith Aviation to Hawker Siddeley Aviation* at Kingston on Thames. I had known John for some years and, when I decided to write a book on Hawker, his enthusiasm and unstinted help knew no bounds.

As I delved deeper my interest was aroused more and more. It developed into a passion and almost a duty to this Australian who achieved so much but is now almost unknown in his own country. I hope this book will help to remedy that situation, and place on record his tremendous contribution to the aviation industry in its very early days.

My wife's involvement with the family remained over the years and this book is the result of her encouragement and support. Her early recollections have helped me capture the atmosphere and feeling of the times.

I have collected the material for this book from many sources. Where original text has been used it has, at times, been given current form of expression, but care has been taken not to disturb the original meaning. Some sections have been directly quoted as I felt it was preferable to preserve the atmosphere of over half a century ago. In a few years there will be no one left alive with personal memories of Hawker and this biography would have been impossible to write. I feel I have been privileged to be able to place this material on record.

Prologue

Shortly before the beginning of World War I Lord Northcliffe, who was the proprietor of the London *Daily Mail*, offered a prize of 10,000 pounds to the first person to fly the Atlantic ocean nonstop. With the outbreak of war it was clearly impossible for anyone to take up this challenge. However, at the cessation of hostilities, Lord Northcliffe renewed the offer. As soon as this was announced Mr T.O.M. Sopwith (popularly known as "Tom" and who later became Sir Thomas Sopwith) notified the Royal Aero Club, who were to conduct the competition, that his firm would be a contender. The natural choice to carry out the attempt was Harry Hawker, who had built up an enormous reputation as a pilot and as an aircraft designer.

After his years of record breaking and test flying Sopwith aircraft during World War I Hawker would have been the most experienced pilot alive at that time. Hawker selected Lt Cdr Mackenzie Grieve, with whom he had been associated during the deck landing trials in the early part of the war, as navigator. A special aircraft was built by the Sopwith Aviation Company (which from now on I will refer to as Sopwiths). This aircraft was named the *Atlantic* and, after testing, it was crated up for transport by ship and rail to St Johns, Newfoundland, from where the flight was to begin.

After the considerable difficulties involved in transporting the aeroplane and finding a suitable field to use, together with a protracted spell of the most foul weather, they were finally able to take off on 18 May 1919. The details of this flight are dealt with in Chapter 9. The epic story of the actual flight, followed by the ditching at sea, is related here in the words of Harry Hawker from his book, *Our Atlantic Attempt.*

"Early on Sunday 18 May the Sopwith *Atlantic* aeroplane was ready, tanks filled, with everything aboard. After saying au revoir to all our friends, we sent our respects to Raynham (who was also waiting for suitable weather to leave from Newfoundland in a Martinsyde aeroplane on a similar attempt).

"After getting the Rolls-Royce engine nicely warmed up and ticking over contentedly, we got in and pushed off at 5.42 pm."

[Some confusion exists about times as the map, from a newspaper, on page 165 shows take-off at 6.48 pm. Hawker's records are likely to be accurate. However it is not clear if his chronometer remained on eastern seaboard time throughout the flight so GMT is also shown.]

"Getting off was just a bit ticklish. The wind was about 20 miles an

Lt Cdr Mackenzie Grieve and Harry Hawker pose beside the fuselage of the Atlantic *before their transatlantic attempt.*

hour east-northeast, which meant that we had to go diagonally across our L shaped ground...and avoiding, if we could, a deep drainage ditch which ran along the foot of it. Our trial flights, both in England and Newfoundland, had been done with a three quarter load of petrol and we knew very well that there would not be too much room to spare on this field with the full load on board.

"However, all was well. The going was rough and the hillside made her roll a bit, but we missed the ditch by inches and got into the air all right with a respectable distance to spare between our wheels and the trees. As soon as we were well up I throttled down and we started a steady climb out towards the Atlantic and towards Ireland that we hoped to see inside the next 24 hours.

"As soon as the coast had been passed, I pulled the undercarriage release trigger and away it went into the water. Simultaneously the needle of the air speed indicator went over to show an increase of 7 miles an hour.

"The sky was bright and clear to start with, but we had not got up many thousand feet, and I think had only been flying about 10 minutes when we saw that Newfoundland's staple product, fog, was hanging on to her coasts. That didn't worry us very much. The fog is never more than a few hundred feet thick and we knew we should soon be leaving it behind. Grieve had been able to observe the sea long enough to get a fair drift reading, and the fog bank didn't interfere with his navigation as it gave him the sort of horizon he wanted, being quite flat and distinct.

"As far as the weather was concerned everything looked quite nice for some hours. We were comfortably jogging along at about 10,000 feet with nothing much in the way of cloud between ourselves and the vault of heaven. The engine was roaring contentedly as though it did not mean to misfire until the tanks were bone dry. The air speed indicator showed a decent cruising speed of 105 miles an hour. There were practically no bumps and I held her on the course that Grieve had laid down.

"At about 10 pm (03.00 GMT) all the blue in the sky had turned to purple, the warm glint of the sun had faded from the polished edges of the struts, and the clouds below us became dull and patchy and grey, only giving us very infrequently a sight of the ocean beneath them.

"A quarter of an hour later the weather conditions had noticeably changed for the worse. The sky became hazy and thick, so that we could not see anything below us with any distinctness, but we could perceive clearly enough that there was some pretty heavy stuff ahead. However, there was only one thing to do. It wasn't very solid so we just poked her nose into it and pushed through, but it was quite decidedly bumpy and now and then a slant of rain would splash on to us. But that didn't matter a bit as we were quite warm and comfortable and were expecting very soon to be able to leave this little patch of nasty weather behind us.

"At about 11 pm (04.00 GMT) I glanced at the water circulation thermometer and saw that it was a good bit higher than it ought to have been, although we were still slightly climbing. It was clear enough that everything was not right with the cooling system, as the temperature did not go down as I expected it to when I opened the shutters over the radiator a little. However, we carried on, but we didn't seem to be able to get free of the clouds which now began to appear thicker and heavier than ever, and there were enough of them at lower levels to prevent any chance of our peeping at the sea.

"By this time we had altered course a little to the northward as, from the information we had received from the meteorological station before starting, we were expecting that the wind would tend to go more into that quarter. But it was none too easy for a decent course to be held, as the cloud formations we were running into were very formidable, and to say the least of it not without bumps. They were too high for us to climb over without wasting a good deal of petrol which we wanted naturally enough to economize in every way. Another reason why we didn't want to climb was the increasing temperature of the water. So we just had to go round the clouds as best we could, but there were so many of them that Grieve never had a chance to take a sight on the stars.

"A little later the moon rose and brightened things up, and the outlook could have done with a bit of brightening. The water temperature in the radiator had risen from 168 degrees to 176 degrees F, in spite of the shutters being quite wide open. It was quite obvious that something serious was amiss, otherwise the Rolls-Royce Eagle engine was running absolutely perfectly, the aeroplane was making no other complaints at all, and Grieve and I were happy and warm enough although the weather was so unkind.

"At about 11.30 pm (04.30 GMT) I determined that something had got to be done to keep the water temperature down. I had reached the conclusion that the most probable cause was a collection of rust and odds and ends of solder and so forth that had shaken loose in the radiator, and were stopping up the filter which prevents any solid substances from getting into the pump.

"Very often one can get rid of this sort of stoppage by stopping the engine and nose diving, so giving the accumulation a chance to spread itself and the filter to clear, with the rust and dirt at the bottom edge of it and not all over it. At any rate, there was nothing else to do, so down went her nose and we dropped quietly from 12,000 to 9,000 feet. I then started the engine up again, and was tremendously relieved to see that the temperature kept moderate although we were soon climbing again. All the same our anxiety was not to be put aside, because if we had to do the clearing process often

Assembling the Atlantic after it had been shipped from England to Newfoundland, Canada. The hangar was specially built for the aircraft under a contract between Monty Fenn and the farmer Andrew Glendenning. This allowed the use of the field for the flight in return for which the hangar became the farmer's property.

A side view of the Sopwith Atlantic *which was specially converted from the Sopwith B1 for the Atlantic Ocean flight.*

it meant that we should waste a lot of petrol which, with the wind a good deal against us, we certainly could not afford to do.

"An hour later, at 12.30 pm, (05.30 GMT) the thermometer had returned to 175 degrees F. We were now about 800 miles out, and the weather had shown no signs whatever of improving, so that we were forced into continuing our cloud dodging tactics. Down went the nose again, but this time our luck did not hold, and when we started to climb up the temperature rose perilously close to boiling point. So we tried again, but things only got worse instead of better and very soon the water started boiling in earnest.

"We had 19 gallons in the engine, but she was pulling about 200 horse power and once she started boiling, in spite of the intense cold (the atmosphere was getting on for zero) I knew it would not take long for the water to evaporate. After the second time of asking I succeeded in getting the machine up to 12,000 feet and throttled her down, so that she would just about stop at that altitude, so as to give the water every chance to cool. The top plane was covered with ice from the radiator and the steam was spouting out like a little geyser

from a tiny hole in the middle of it. For some little time we were able to keep the temperature just a little below the fateful 212 degrees F.

"There was now not much difficulty about keeping a course for the moon was well up, and our 12,000 feet took us above most of the clouds, so that now and then Grieve was able to take an observation on the stars which peeped out through gaps, mostly to the northward. About 6 am (11.00 GMT) we found ourselves confronted with a bank of black clouds as solid as a range of mountains and rearing themselves up in fantastic and menacing formations. They were at least 15,000 feet high, so it was obviously useless to try and get over the top of them, but when we couldn't fly round them. Going through them was out of the question, after we had one try at it we had a shot at going over some of the lower ones. Each time we climbed the water temperature rose and began to boil furiously. So it was no good going on with that scheme.

"In the meantime I had no other trouble whatever in flying the machine as she was quite easy to trim and, when we got engulfed in the blackness of the clouds every now and then, one was able to keep

(Upper) This is almost certainly a picture taken just before take-off on the Atlantic attempt. The splayed position of the wheels indicates the heavy load the aeroplane was carrying. Note also the "dolly" supporting the tail which helped shorten the take-off. The engine appears to be going flat out with helpers holding back the plane until it was at full throttle.

(Lower) The Atlantic taking off on a test flight. This was the same field they were to use for their final departure. Note the hills in the background which Hawker only just cleared because of the heavy fuel load he carried on the actual day.

her level with the compass and the bubble.

"Very reluctantly we came to the conclusion that as we couldn't go up we should have to come down, so we descended to about 6,000 feet at about 6 am (11.00 GMT). Here it was blacker than ever, so we continued our descent further and at about 1,000 feet found things a good deal brighter with the cheerful sun just getting up to help us on our way.

"Grieve's observations on the stars had shown that we were now on our course and well inside the steamer lane.

"Water that constantly boiled even at 1,000 feet did not help matters, and what showed us that we had really lost a great deal (if only we could have slung a bucket over board and picked up a few gallons as we went along!) was the fact that in our descent we had a very narrow squeak indeed. No sooner had the engine stopped than it must have gone stone cold owing to the small amount of water left in the jackets, though steam was coming out of the radiator relief pipe quite merrily for some little time. This fact we had not realized until, when quite low down, I opened the throttle and got no response whatever.

"I then shouted to Grieve to get busy on the petrol pump, and he was very soon bending forward and pumping hard enough to push the carburettor needle valves right off their seats and flooding the jets with petrol.

"Nothing happened at all except that the Atlantic rose up to meet us at rather an alarming rate. We were gliding down wind at a pretty good speed, the sea was very rough and when we hit it I knew very well that there was going to be a crash of sorts and that, if he remained where he was, Grieve would probable get badly damaged as he would be shot forward head first on to the petrol tank. I clumped him hard on the back and yelled to him that I was going to land.

"We were then about 10 feet above the particularly uninviting looking waves when we had the biggest stroke of luck.

"Thanks to Grieve's pumping the engine at last fired, I gave her a good mouthful of throttle and she roared away with the best will in the world, the dive flattened, tilted into a climb and we were soon back again to a four figure altitude and very glad to be there.

"Had we hit the water we should have had not the slightest hope. Probably we would have been hurt owing to our speed with the wind, the aeroplane would have been badly damaged, and it was ten to one that if we had sense enough left to launch the boat we shouldn't have been able to use it and there was every probability of it being all over with us pretty quickly. I for one do not want a narrower shave.

"By this time we had come to the conclusion that nothing could be gained by going on; we could still fly for an hour or two with what water we had left, but to get to Ireland was no longer within the range of practical consideration; we had plenty of petrol, but the depletion of the water was what was critical. We decided shortly after 6 am (11.00 GMT) to wander round in search of a ship. For this purpose we steered a sort of zigzag course, dodging the clouds and squalls of rain, being forced to keep down low owing to the clouds.

"If we didn't spot a ship, then we had simply to make the best landing we could, launch the boat, touch off our big Holmes flare which would last for an hour at least, and hope for the best. We also had plenty of Very lights to fall back upon, and if it turned out to be a long job we had plenty of food for we had scarcely touched any on the flight beyond drinking a fair amount of coffee and munching chocolate. Neither of us as a matter of fact had felt like eating at all.

"We flew around for some two hours or so in weather that was getting a good deal worse rather than better. There was no lack of rain squalls, the wind was getting stronger and gustier and bumpier every minute, and the sea rougher. I was very glad to be without the undercarriage, and would rather have been as I was than have floats under me, for the waves looked too heavy for any ordinary seaplane to land.

"As may be imagined, I was not altogether without anxiety although I knew we were right on the steamer route, to which we had taken care to shape our course, because there was plenty of fog and we might have passed quite close to a ship without seeing her.

"Suddenly a hull loomed out of the fog and we knew that our luck, if it had been patchy, was at least good enough to stand up when the big strain came on it. I am ready to admit that I shouted with joy, Grieve says he felt like doing the same thing, but evidently the tradition of the Silent Service (to which he is an ornament) was too much for his vocal chords.

"The hull belonged to the good ship *Mary* of Denmark, and she was sailing towards, for us, home. We flew around her and fired three Very light distress signals and kept close by until her crew began to appear on the decks. Then we pushed off a couple of miles or so along her course, judged the wind from the wave crests, came round into it and made a cushy landing in spite of the high sea that was running. The machine alighted quite nicely and, thanks to her partly empty tanks, rode clear of the water, although now and then the waves sloshed right over it and us and soon played havoc with the main planes.

"We had no difficulty in detaching our emergency boat and getting it launched, for the machine was sinking pretty fast, although we did not expect it would be likely to go down altogether. Our life saving suits worked splendidly and kept us quite dry. The *Mary* was soon close up to us and made speed to get a lifeboat out, but although she was only 200 yards off it was an hour and a half before she could get to us and take us off. They had run a line out to the boat from the ship

A painting of the dramatic rescue of Hawker and Grieve, by a lifeboat from the SS Mary, *after they were forced to ditch in mid Atlantic.*

and we were soon hauled in. Owing to the heavy sea it was impossible for us to salvage anything but, as we now know, a good part of the machine and the mail bag was afterwards picked up by the steamship *Lake Charlotteville* and brought into Falmouth, so that our letters were delivered after all.

"We were picked up on Monday at 8.30 am (13.30 GMT), rather wet and tired, fourteen and a half hours after we had started from Newfoundland.

"Neither Grieve nor myself can possibly find words to express our deep gratitude to Captain Duhn of the good ship *Mary*. His men had extreme difficulty in taking us off, and we owe our lives to their gallantry, for there is no doubt that, as Captain Duhn said, in another hour we should have gone down for keeps.

"We had hoped to fall in with a ship equipped with wireless so that we could communicate with our people in England and of this Captain Duhn, who spoke excellent English, thought we had a good chance, but later on the storm got considerably worse and he had to heave to, only making very little way in a northerly direction and so going further away from the busier shipping route. It was not until we were off the Butt of Lewis that we could communicate with home and the world, which at one time had seemed so distant, that we were safe and sound.

"The destroyer *Woolston* picked us up outside Loch Erriboll and took us to Scapa Flow, where we received a wonderful welcome from the Grand Fleet and Admiral Fremantle.

"The next day we were put on terra firma and made the best of our way home. As to the reception we received and the demonstrations that were made, need I say that Grieve and I were more than deeply touched. We are completely agreed that the whole of this business was utterly undeserved and out of all proportion to what we had tried, and failed to do.

"The men who should have the reception are Raynham and Morgan, for what they did was a magnificent act of pluck. The east-northeast wind was not by any means a bad one for our getting off, for it suited our aerodrome pretty much as well as any other and better than most, but it was almost the worst possible wind for the Martinsyde aerodrome. Knowing this Raynham and Morgan never hesitated to attempt the flight, and in doing so they displayed a spirit and a courage for which Grieve and I have nothing but the most intense admiration and respect. They were visited with cruel hard luck indeed."

The first pilot to attempt a flight across the Atlantic from Newfoundland to Ireland: Mr Harry George Hawker.

Chapter One

Early Days

Harry George Hawker was born on 22 January 1889 on the shores of Port Phillip in the little village of Moorabbin, now a suburb of Melbourne in the State of Victoria, Australia.

His father, George Hawker, was born at Harcourt in Victoria on 10 January 1862. He had a blacksmith's and wheelwright's shop at South Brighton and this was where the young Harry Hawker developed his early interest in engineering and gained some practical knowledge.

George Hawker had married Mary Ann Gilliard Anderson on 24 May 1883. She was born at Stawell, Victoria, on 9 October 1859. There were four children; Maude, Herbert, Harry and Ruby.

Some years later Maude married A.W. Chamberlain who was in the motor business. They had two sons, Alan Hawker Chamberlain born on 16 July 1908 and Howard Francis Chamberlain born on 25 June 1910.

The following account of events in which the Hawker family were involved during the early days has been set down by A.H. (Bob) Chamberlain, whose extraordinary recall of his early memories have made this biography possible. In addition he has been the source of many of the photographs.

"Harry went to the Worthing Road State School where there is a plaque commemorating his attendance. It was erected in 1922. This school was quite near to Harry's father's business which, at the time, was on the corner of Wyckham Road and Nepean Highway, Moorabbin. At this period the area was known as South Brighton.

"Harry, also for a time, attended the Brighton Road State School. There seems to be an oft-repeated statement that he disliked school and often ran away. This needs some qualification. He did have some brief ventures to other schools but eventually decided that the Worthing Road School suited him best. Although he left school before he reached the regular State School leaving age of 14 years, he had in fact completed the course and reached the normal standard required of 14 year olds.

"Harry always got along well with his parents, respecting their high standards of duty and discipline. The Hawker home was a hive of activity. Living in Moorabbin they were surrounded by lush

George Hawker, Harry's father, dressed in the uniform of Sergeant of the Victorian Field Artillery.

Mary Ann Hawker, Harry's mother.

*(Upper) Harry as a cadet at the age of 12.
Most schools ran cadet corps at this time
as a way of developing discipline.*

MOORABBIN S.S. Nº 1111
ERECTED IN COMMEMORATION OF
THE FAMOUS AVIATOR
HARRY HAWKER
A PAST PUPIL OF THIS SCHOOL
KILLED 12-7-21

There are two Moorabbin State Schools in the South Brighton area. (Lower) The one on Worthing Road was known as the Worthing Road State School and was the school that Harry attended. (Upper) It still has the plaque dedicated to Harry Hawker.

paddocks and kept a couple of cows and a few riding horses.

"Harry's father, George Hawker, was born at Harcourt, Victoria in 1862. His mother Rosanna had come to Australia as a one year old child with her parents, Thomas and Eleanor Calcutt, in 1842.

"The Calcutts had been shepherds in Sussex, England, and were part of a group of migrants who came out to Australia to work on an estate at Brighton. During their long voyage their sponsor had lost favour with the Australian government and his rights to a very large area of land and financially assisted migrant labour had not been confirmed. When the Calcutt family arrived at Brighton by bullock wagon, they learned that they had neither work nor accommodation.

"Australia was an undeveloped country of harsh environment in 1842 but the Calcutts were tough and managed to survive; Thomas Calcutt later being listed as a carpenter and raised his family at Taradale, Victoria. The daughter married James Henry Hawker and, after their son George Hawker was born, Henry died. Rosanna later married a blacksmith named Ryan who taught his stepson George the trades of blacksmith and wheelwright. Obviously he taught him thoroughly because George became skilled at working both wood and metal.

"At Harcourt, Victoria, George Hawker married Mary Ann Gilliard Anderson, a dressmaker whose father was a blacksmith. They moved to Moorabbin where George Hawker set up in business and they raised their family of two boys and two girls. George Hawker always worked extremely hard and brought the family up in a tradition of personal activity. They milked the cows, made their own cream and butter and baked their own bread. Fowls were kept for eggs and chicken dinners, and they grew some vegetables. George Hawker just couldn't tolerate idleness in any form and if any project reached a doubtful situation would say, 'Don't stand around doing nothing, do something, even if it is wrong.'

"George Hawker was a first class rifle shot and successful in many competitions. George became a member of the Victorian Rifle Association in 1890 and also served in the militia as a Farrier Sgt in C Battery of the Victorian Field Artillery. He was a member of the Australian Rifle Team sent to England in mid 1897, and again in 1898, to compete at Bisley. This Australian team won the Kolapore Cup in 1897 and were runners up only a few points behind the winning team, in 1898.

"The long trip by steamship in those early days meant George Hawker was away from his family and his business for quite significant periods in mid 1897 and 1898 when Harry (born in January 1889) would have been 8 or 9 years old.

"The other members of the Hawker family were, the eldest my mother Maude, then Herbert and, after Harry, Ruby who would have been a baby at that time. Much effort was spent by George Hawker on noncommercial projects but the family, in their healthy active way, enjoyed life.

"George Hawker's business was general blacksmithing and wagon building. He built covered wagons for the local market gardeners to transport their goods to market. At this time and up to the 1930s, the structure of Nepean Highway, which ran past the Hawker shop, was rather unusual. On one side of the wide highway was a special track for the market wagons which travelled through the early hours of the mornings and returned in the evenings. This track consisted of two metal rails each about 12 inches wide with side flanges raised about 1 inch. These rails were spaced at the standard width for the wheeltracks of the wagons. Between the metal tracks, and for about 2 feet each side, the roadway comprised bluestone pitchers (cobblestones). The remainder of the road was macadam. The market gardeners, many of them Chinese, drove the horse into the centre section of the pitchers and the iron- tyred wheels ran in the steel channels. The driver then went to sleep and the horse plodded through the night right into the city of Melbourne. When the driver woke up he continued through the city streets to the market to sell his fruit and vegetables. He returned by the same route in the evening. The design of the wagons became, to some extent, standardized and they were built by many other workshops similar to George Hawker's.

"Although trained as a blacksmith and wheelwright, George Hawker had a good sense of engineering on a much wider base. He designed and built the two cylinder vertical steam engine and boiler which provided the power for his shop. This engine would be of about 5 or 6 hp and was a normal slide valve double acting type with water feed pump and flyball governor. The boiler was of standard vertical fire tube design. I remember it well and it gave a satisfactory performance. When the Hawker shop was set up on a reduced basis behind their house in Gourlay Street, Balaclava, I lived with them for some time, including the period when Harry stayed there during his 1914 visit. George Hawker had to get up very early to attend the fire at the boiler when the power was required for a day's work.

"My father, Bert Chamberlain, later was to tell me how George Hawker had built this engine and boiler. He bought a lathe, which he still had when I lived with them, and set it up for drive by pedals. It was quite a large lathe for pedal power and must have called for much muscular effort. He made the patterns for the engine castings and had the parts cast by Paynes Foundry at the corner of Elizabeth and Victoria Streets in the city. He forged the crankshaft and connecting rods then machined them all by pedal power. Building the engine and boiler by primitive methods must have been a mammoth task. The rivet holes in the boiler were drilled by a hand powered post drill as found in most old time blacksmith shops. Holes which

A Cottin-Desgouttes car owned by Harry's father. Harry is standing on the far side; Bob Chamberlain is seated.

Harry Hawker at the wheel of a 1910 Argyll. He had grown a moustache and is dressed for the occasion.

34

couldn't be reached by the post drill were drilled using a ratchet drill requiring great physical effort.

"Harry, as a young boy, would have seen all this procedure and would, as I was in later years, be taken by George Hawker to other and better workshops to see at first hand the skills of the period. Some few years later Harry was to build his own small petrol engine to power his workshop. He had to use the same methods but his task was simple compared with his father's earlier effort.

"In 1900 George Hawker built a steam car which unfortunately, in later years, became something of a family joke. It was a lightweight vehicle obviously copied from the small Stanley or Locomobile of the period. Built with crude machinery, it was not a success. The engine was under the single seat and drove by a single exposed chain to the differential in the centre of the rear axle assembly. The remains of this early steamer were still around when I lived with the Hawker family and I remember such items as the small bevel type differential with sun and planet pinions cast in bronze with teeth filed up from castings.

"I was told many years later, by my mother, that George Hawker would set off proudly down the road under a good head of steam but would return from the journeys, which were all short, pushing the car. When the power plant failed he would remove the joining link from the driving chain and start pushing. His family loved him dearly but all, including my very loyal and proud mother, regarded the steam car as a joke. After the steam car George Hawker built a single cylinder horizontal steam engine of about 6 inches bore to power a sawmill. He also built the horizontal boiler for this engine.

"Of course he had his own steam engine for his workshop at this time but building this relatively large steam plant with his minimal machinery meant that such fitting work as installing the cylinder on the bedplate had to be done with cold chisel and file. When the sawmill was abandoned many years later I was able to examine this steam plant. The boiler at some time had been allowed to prime and water had got into the cylinder resulting in the engine bedplate being broken right across the centre. It had been repaired by bolting steel plates across the break but I don't know if George Hawker was called on to do this repair or if it was done by the sawmill operator.

"Harry Hawker's father was a man of action working long hard hours over a wide range of interests. He had his rifle club activities at Williamstown across the bay involving tram, train and small steamboat trips and a long walk each way every time he went to the shooting range. He was deeply religious and involved in Church affairs. No matter how hard he worked during the week or how urgent a job may be there was no way George Hawker would do any work on a Sunday, visiting the Methodist Church, morning and evening, with all the family.

Harry leaning on the Argyll in the garage De Little built on his property at Caramut. Note the long-bed, treadle-driven, lathe. He would have used this when he built his motorcycles.

"Such was the background in which Harry grew up. It was a time when very hard work for the necessities of life was normal for most families in Australia. However it was an engineering environment. The workshop equipment was crude but George Hawker was a master craftsman in both wood and metal.

"He must have been patient and kind hearted because he would take me to the city before I was 6 years old. A typical trip by train and tram would be to Tinsleys where he would select such parts for wagons as axleboxes, which would be later delivered by horse lorry, then on to Royals where we would watch forgings being made under steam hammers. Sometimes we would go to Kellow Falkiners where they had car agencies and one of the best workshops in Melbourne. I would see them grinding crankshafts in a big lathe using throwblocks and a big toolpost grinder.

"One day I remember watching mechanics repairing a German Phanomobile which had its four cylinder air-cooled engine mounted up on top of the single front wheel. We agreed that this was a pretty poor way to build a car. This three wheeled car still exists today. We would go to Paynes iron foundry and watch very skillful molders making molds for complex castings, sometimes using strickle board, square and rule with a degree of skill not used in this field today.

"It is certain that Harry had, at a very early age, the opportunity to see light engineering work being carried out by skilled craftsmen in many areas of the industry. Perhaps it is understandable that he wanted to get school behind him and start practical work. Later he regretted having only a State School level of mathematics and, during the war when he was working on aircraft design, wrote in a letter to my mother that he had started a course at night school to try and overcome some of the disabilities of limited academic knowledge. It is doubtful if he ever had the time to achieve much in this area and there were others around who already had the training. Harry never really let his level of schooling restrict his activities and never let it lower his confidence in what he was doing.

"Harry's friends around the 1908 to 1911 period, Harry Busteed, Harry Kauper, Cecil De Fraga and others, including my father Bert Chamberlain, were all skilled mechanics and were interested in the great new challenge of cars, motorcycles and aeroplanes. Harry Busteed had already built a high-powered motorcycle and later built a still larger one.

"Harry Hawker started work at Hall and Warden where they made bicycles and invalid chairs in their workshop at the corner of Sturt Street and City Road, South Melbourne. They also had a subagency for De Dion cars. His work there didn't give him the opportunity he wanted and for a short period he went to work at The Tarrant Motor Company where Colonel Harley Tarrant had built several complete cars.

"Next was a job as chauffeur mechanic on a grazing property owned by Mr McBean at Deniliquin, just over the border in New South Wales. He enjoyed this job but left to go to Skipton in the Western District of Victoria and work for Mr Ernest Austin at his property *Borriyallock*. He was really chasing opportunities to get more experience with different types of cars and his next job was most rewarding. He went to work as chauffeur mechanic for Mr Ernest De Little at Caramut. There was real opportunity here. Mr De Little was about to buy a new Argyle car and Harry was sent down to the Melbourne agents to collect it. Harry kept detailed log books for this car as he did for the next new car he collected for Mr De Little, a Rolls-Royce Silver Ghost tourer. The log books show that Harry drove the De Little cars about 20,000 miles per year and over the period of about 3 years until 1911 the only trouble he had was with tyres. One of the driving log books was a school exercise book and on the front cover were printed areas for students to fill in showing their level of schooling. By the lines marked 'Class' and 'Year' Harry had filled in 'First Class' 'Any Year', showing the good sense of humour which he always displayed.

"Harry, like his father, was a fine rifle shot and this interest was shared by Mr De Little who also was an expert. They had this common interest and got along very well together. The home on the big De Little property was *Caramut House* and De Little had a good reputation as a fair employer who took a kindly interest in the work people on his property, giving them Christmas and birthday gifts. The governess for the De Little children told me many years later how all the staff enjoyed life at *Caramut*.

"Mr De Little paid Harry 200 pounds per year wages and also paid his board at the local hotel so that he did not have to live in the staff quarters. The hotel was just across the road from the home. It was owned by the McPhee family and when Harry left to go to England in 1911 Mrs McPhee took out an insurance policy on him and kept this insurance active right up to the time of his death. A small amount, but an act of warm friendship.

"Harry's older brother, Bert, also worked in the Western District as chauffeur mechanic on another large grazing property. Bert had a different temperament to Harry and little is known of his early life. He apparently enjoyed school and studied well having a strong sense of duty. His health was not robust but he inherited some mechanical expertise and tenacity from his parents in the same environment as Harry. Bert was driving for the Afflecks and had his own single cylinder 'Sizaire Naudin' car which he frequently drove to Melbourne to see his parents. Bert got his motor car driving licence on the first day licences were issued in Victoria. He went to World War I as a sergeant, was at Gallipoli, and served right through to the end of the war in France, coming home with the rank of captain and a

Military Cross.

"His never robust health had suffered a further setback when he was in an area which was gassed. Bert got leave from France to go to England for Harry's wedding and spent a little time again in England after the war when many Australian servicemen were over there awaiting transport home. In spite of health problems Bert worked right up to the start of World War II but died in Caulfield Military Hospital.

"A very minor, but amusing situation, occurred in the 1920s when Bert bought two ABC motor scooters. They had been designed by Granville Bradshaw, who had also designed the engine with which Harry had won the Michelin Cup endurance contest in 1912 with a flight at Brooklands of 8 hours 23 minutes. Harry always regarded Granville Bradshaw as a great engine designer, (a view not universally accepted), so Bert considered that these motor scooters must be good. To ride one of these small-wheeled light machines in the rough environment of Melbourne in those early days required real bravery. Kids and grown men would catcall and yell out what they considered were witty derisive statements. This situation didn't last long because the machines were utterly unreliable and Bert gave them to my brother who was then a schoolboy. Brother Bill learned a lot about how not to build an engine from these machines. Like many other Bradshaw projects they were pioneering efforts, ahead of their time, which were never properly developed.

"Ernest De Little had the workshop built for Harry and as Harry's only official work was to drive and maintain two well built new cars, he had plenty of time for his own work as there was very little else to do. Harry bought a lathe and like his father had done years earlier set it up for pedal power. He had plenty of helpers to do the pedalling. He designed a single cylinder water-cooled horizontal engine generally similar to thousands of small petrol engines being used on country properties at that time. Cooling was by thermosiphon from a water tank. Overhead valves were used, the intake valve being of the atmospheric (automatic) type. Main bearing supports were in one piece with the main base and the cylinder held on with flanges set screwed to facings cast on the base and filed flat to fit related facings also filed flat on the cylinder casting. Lubrication was by a screw down grease cup on the big end bearing and drip feed lubricators for cylinder and main bearings. Carburettor and magneto were bought in. The connecting rod was marine type and all parts were designed so that they could be built with the minimal equipment available. The forgings for crankshaft and connecting rod were probably made by Harry's father who also arranged for castings to be made from patterns brought down by Harry, who drove the De Littles to Melbourne fairly often. Harry, at that early age, must have had the ability to make the basic drawings necessary.

The Caramut Hotel where Harry lived while working for Ernest De Little. Harry is not in the photograph, but the first motorcycle he made is leaning against the wall of the hotel.

"The engine was completed and the workshop set up so that he could get on with doing what he really wanted to do, build a motorcycle. He did, in fact, build two motorcycles. At that time, of course, motorcycles were simple machinery compared with today's complicated and highly developed precision masterpieces.

"Available from parts importers were such items as wheel rims, frame fittings, drive belt rims etc. It was usual for even large makers of motorcycles to buy these parts from specialist suppliers and the ingenuity was usually displayed in assembling a well selected group of parts. A wide range of engines was available but Harry completely designed and built his own engines. His first motorcycle had a V twin cylinder engine of modest size. This unit was built to a normal specification of the period and had side exhaust valves in pockets beside the air-cooled cylinders and the automatic (atmospheric) intake valves were located above the exhaust's valves. Drive from engine to rear wheel was by means of a simple V belt. This system was at the time in general use.

"To start the machine the rider ran along pushing it by the handlebars with the engine rotating freely because the exhaust valves were held off their seats by a valve lifter built into the design. It was operated by a handgrip lever working through a Bowden flexible cable and casing. There was nothing unusual about this machine. It was like many medium powered motorcycles of the period, simple and reliable. Harry showed his advanced thinking in making this first machine with a two cylinder engine. There were other similar machines around with twin engines but most had even simpler single cylinder power.

"Harry's next project was a much more ambitious one, a really high-powered racing motorcycle, with a very large two cylinder engine. At this period the J.A. Prestwich Company (JAP) in England, had built the biggest racing motorcycle engine so far built in Britain. Harry had obviously seen photos of this 20 hp engine because the one he built for his own racing machine had many features copied from the JAP which was raced in England fitted to Matchless and NLG machines.

"The two enormous cylinders of the JAP were set at 90 degrees which they believed gave better running balance but made installation rather cumbersome. While copying the main features, Harry built his engine with similar huge cylinders but set at the more convenient, and usual, 60 degrees making for a more compact installation. Both intake and exhaust valves were in the cylinder heads and all were operated by rocker arms and pushrods. He made the complete engine, including the carburettor, which was obviously inspired by the JAP design. Ignition was by dry batteries and coils. The high tension coils were of French manufacture and must have given a lot of trouble because there were several faulty used coils amongst the parts he left behind when he went to England in 1911.

"Drive was by a V belt direct from engine to rear wheel using a very large pulley on the engine to give high speed gearing. He made several of these drive pulleys of different diameters so that he could get the desired drive ratio by changing pulleys. These pulleys were machined all over and were extremely thin at the outer part indicating that Harry had an appreciation of weight effect. The flywheels were inside the crankcase as with normal motorcycle engines. There was no silencing system, each exhaust port being directed downward by an elbow and a short pipe parallel to its cylinder. Coils and dry batteries for ignition were, at first, carried in a small box mounted at the tip of the unsprung front fork just above the tyre, but other locations were later tried for these parts. Weight was cut to a minimum on every part.

"My father, who had ridden the machine, told me many years later that the performance was rough but very good for the time and Harry raced this machine against his friends Harry Busteed and Cecil De Fraga who also built their own machines. Busteed's machine had enormous cylinders but used a simpler side valve design. They raced on a steeply banked wooden track which was built for racing pedal cycles, located in St Kilda Road near Flinders Street Railway Station, where the Arts Centre now stands. The track was only an eighth of a mile and the high-powered rough running motorcycles soon started to shake the wooden structure to pieces. They were then barred from using this track so raced on the country roads.

"When Harry went to England in 1911 he left the racing motorcycle in a shed at his parents' home where it stayed until he returned with the Sopwith Tabloid biplane in 1914. He did not use the machine during his visit and just before leaving to return to England he was approached on the ship by a man who offered him 60 pounds for it. This was quite a lot of money for any motorcycle in 1914. Harry accepted the offer and handed the money straight over to his mother. She later died of cancer on 21 April 1917 while her two sons were still overseas involved in the war.

"While working for Mr De Little in 1910 Harry had taken some time off to go to Diggers Rest, in Victoria, to see the first controlled flight by a full sized powered aircraft in Australia. With him was Harry Busteed, Harry Kauper and my father, Bert Chamberlain. They all camped on the Diggers Rest Railway Station to be near at hand when flights were attempted. The aircraft on the paddock could only be flown when climatic conditions were suitable and nobody could be sure of when this would occur. A wait of perhaps several days was a possibility and then it was likely that best flying conditions would be in the early morning.

"Two pilots were there so it was a case of who would get into the air

(Left) Hawker and Cecil de Fraga racing on the board track which had been built for bicycles at Princes Park, Melbourne (1910).

(Lower left) Cecil de Fraga, another of Harry Hawker's motorcycle racing friends, with his V twin Buchet, photographed in 1909 at Princes Park raceway.

(Lower) The motorcycle Harry Busteed built and raced with Harry Hawker. The rider had to sit over the rear wheel and use long handlebars because the engine was so large.

Houdini (Erlich Weiss) flying his French Voisin aeroplane, powered by a 60 hp English ENV engine, in 1910 at Diggers Rest, near Melbourne. This was the first recorded flight in Australia. The photo was taken by Bert Hawker.

first. Erlich Weiss, whose stage name was Houdini, a world famed escapologist, had his Voisin biplane. He had learned to fly in France and was accompanied by a French mechanic. The other pilot was Colin De Fries who was to fly a Wright biplane owned by a Mr Adamson, the Head of Wesley College. He had imported this plane and also an Anzani powered Bleriot monoplane. The Wright had been built in France under licence to the famous Wright brothers, Wilbur and Orville. It was powered by a 25 hp engine designed by the Wrights and a mechanic who was employed by them.

"An unusual set of circumstances had led up to the production of this aircraft. Following their short flights at Kitty Hawk in 1903 the Wrights had avoided publicity while they improved their aircraft at Dayton. By 1905 it was fairly established in USA that the Wrights were making reasonably long well-controlled flights from a field near their Dayton, Ohio workshop but still resisted all efforts by interested parties to see what they were doing. There has never been any satisfactory explanation for their secrecy but they were trying to sell aircraft to the USA Government with little success.

"Their now generally accepted achievements were, at that period, doubted in Europe but a Paris newspaper persuaded Wilbur Wright to bring an aircraft to France, and demonstrate it. He took an aircraft to France but locked it in a shed at Le Mans where it stayed for almost a year while the doubters became even more convinced that Wright couldn't do what he had claimed. There has never been any real explanation for the continued reluctance to let people see what they had, but it seems to have been related to controversial patent activity over their system of using wing-warping for lateral stability.

"During the period when the plane was locked away, always with Wilbur Wright in attendance, it had been arranged for Short Brothers to make copies of this aircraft in England and a further license was arranged for some to be built in France. Also during this period the engine was removed and taken to the established engine building firm of Barraquand and Marre in Paris where it was dismantled and drawings made of every part. This was necessary as the Wright engine had been hand built from very sketchy drawings. Barraquand and Marre built a small batch of the engines under a license agreement with the Wrights and it is one of these engines which was fitted to the Wright bought by Mr Adamson. The engine was number 15 and I was fortunate in being able, many years later, to secure it for the Melbourne Science Museum where it is at the present time. The Wright plane at Le Mans, like the very first Wright, had no undercarriage but ran on a trolley along rails and was assisted by a falling weight with cable and pulley arrangement. The Short Brothers and French versions differed in being equipped with wheels for taking off and landing.

Hawker and Busteed set sail for England on the SS Otranto.

"When, after all the delay and doubt, Wilbur Wright brought his machine out of its shed at Le Mans he confounded all his critics by putting up a better flying performance than expected. He showed a degree of control far better than had been anticipated and had no difficulty getting airborne or landing on his skids. The engine had problems after some flights and was replaced by one of those built by Barraquand and Marre.

"De Freis, with the French built Wright, and Houdini, with the Voisin, waited for suitable flying conditions at Diggers Rest. De Freis, who had the benefit of one flying lesson from Captain Ferber in France, was the first to decide that conditions were suitable. The engine was run up, the plane ran along and before gaining sufficient flying speed, was pulled up into a stall and crashed to the ground. De Freis was first to be airborne but only for seconds. Houdini waited for better flying conditions then made successful flights in the Voisin. This was a much more powerful machine than the Wright and had a 60 hp V8 engine built by the ENV Company. Houdini persuaded De Freis to sign a document agreeing that he, Houdini, had made the first flight.

"The small group of enthusiasts had received full value for the hardship of camping on the Diggers Rest railway station. Harry Busteed had already booked his voyage to England. Harry Hawker and Harry Kauper decided to go with him. My father had been able to take pictures of the Voisin on the ground and in the air.

"Harry's ambition to learn to fly was not likely to be realised in Australia as flying was in its infancy. The sight of a very early Wright and a Bleriot aircraft no doubt stirred this urge further. Hawker had saved about 100 pounds and quickly decided to go with Busteed when a berth was found on the ship. He felt that his ambition to learn to fly would be much more easily satisfied in England. He was full of self-confidence, and the fact that he would undoubtedly meet stiff competition did not cause him any misgivings."

Chapter Two

Learning to Fly

Hawker, together with the three other Australians, Busteed, Kauper and Harrison, finally arrived by ship in England in May 1911. All four were eventually destined for careers in the aeronautical field. When they arrived in London, Hawker and Kauper looked around for accommodation that was within their means, in order to give them time to find their feet and look for suitable jobs.

They spent a couple of weeks seeing the sights and then the serious search for work began. Their confidence was severely tested as this did not turn out to be as easy as they expected. Jobs in the engineering field were not plentiful and their position was more difficult as they had no references and found resistance amongst employers because of this. This was unsettling as they would not have had any difficulty in finding work in Australia.

In desperation Hawker offered to work for any prospective employer for a week, for nothing, so that his ability could be assessed. The outlook was most discouraging and before long he and Kauper were forced to move into cheaper lodgings. By this time their funds were running low and they were barely able to afford the necessities of life. They knew no one in the country but maintained their optimism and were careful in their letters home to put on a cheerful front and not to reveal the true state of their affairs or the problems they were having.

After two bad months Hawker's fortune changed. On 29 July 1911 he landed a job with the Commer Company at the rate of sevenpence per hour. It was a meagre beginning but it gave them hope that in the long run they would succeed in landing worthwhile jobs. The search for a better position continued.

On 22 January 1912 Hawker moved to the Mercedes Company at ninepence halfpenny per hour. He stayed with this firm for two months before moving to the Austro Daimler Company on 18 March. These were pretty small beginnings, but at least it enabled him to survive and to build up a reputation amongst local employers.

Whenever Harry had some time off he visited Brooklands to watch the flying as this was, at that time, the centre of aviation in England. All the aeroplanes being built in England were made there and most of the flying took place there. Frequent damage to the aeroplanes

Brooklands Track — 1913

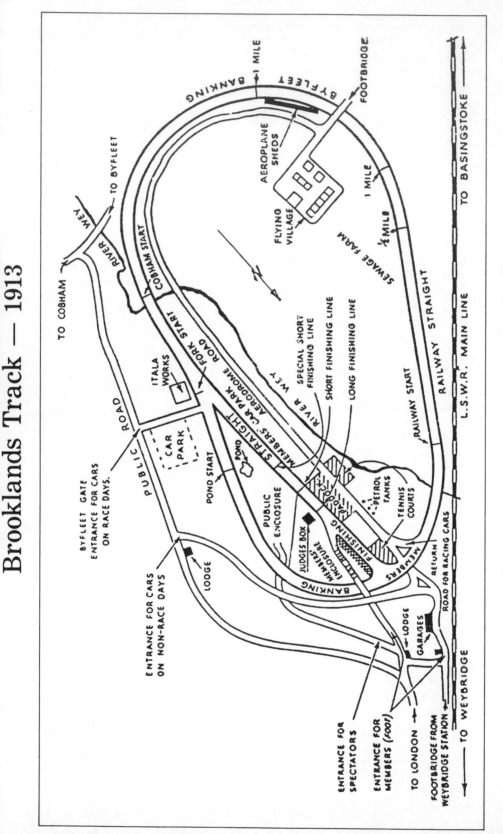

Brooklands Race Track in 1913. The Clubhouse was below the Judges' Box.

necessitated that both of these activities were close together. The possibility of ever reaching a position where he could learn to fly seemed remote because of the competition from other like-minded young men. He did, however, gain a lot of valuable experience and his burning ambition never wavered. There was always the chance that an opportunity would present itself.

Kauper had fared no better in trying to secure employment and was still out of work when he saw an advertisement for a mechanic with Sopwiths, who were building aircraft in addition to running a flying school. He immediately applied and was successful. This proved to be just the kind of work that both he and Hawker were looking for.

After he had been there for about a week Sopwiths secured some orders which meant that they had to increase their work force. Kauper immediately sent Hawker a telegram telling him that the prospects for employment were good and advised him to get down there as soon as possible.

Hawker resigned from his job with the Austro Daimler Company, packed his gear, and proceeded posthaste to Brooklands, never dreaming that this was to be the major turning point in his life. Kauper had recommended Hawker to Mr F. Sigrist, the Works Manager, so when Hawker turned up with his bag and tool kit for the interview, he was immediately put on the pay roll on 29 June 1912.

It did not take Sigrist long to find out that he had secured a very good man. Hawker was hard-working, very quick and accurate, and could handle any job given to him. He worked long hours, seven days a week, for very little pay. For the first time since he had arrived in England he was able to put all the disappointment and frustration behind him and soon built up a reputation as a first-rate mechanic.

He now took the precaution of saving 50 pounds from his wages as a reserve to pay his fare home should he be unable to find further work!

Sopwiths were running a flying school in conjunction with the factory at that time. One day Hawker asked Tom Sopwith if he would teach him to fly. In reply to Tom Sopwith's question as to what would happen if he broke the aeroplane, Harry took from inside his sock the money he had saved for his fare home and asked if it would cover any damage!

Hawker's great ambition was at long last beginning to materialize. One of the problems was getting his hands on an aeroplane. The school had only four aeroplanes at that time: a Burgess Wright dual control machine; a Howard Wright; a Sopwith Farman; and a 70 hp Bleriot for more advanced flying. There were several pupils and, naturally, there was a lot of competition for their use. After doing some taxiing on the aerodrome Hawker, at last, arranged to fly at 7.00 am one morning.

(Upper left) An interesting photograph, taken from a radio-controlled model plane, by John Crampton. It shows Brooklands as it is today and was taken to celebrate Sir Thomas Sopwith's 100th birthday.

(Lower left) A photo by John Crampton showing the Judges' Box and Clubhouse in 1988. (Lower) The Brooklands Track as it looked in 1988.

Harry Hawker, flying the Grasshopper at very low level round the Brooklands Race Track, passes under the bridge that led to the Sopwith sheds on the right.

In those days instructional flights were of short duration, from five to ten minutes, but it was not long before his natural aptitude for flying became apparent and just four days after his first lesson he was considered safe enough to fly the Sopwith Farman solo. When this took place early one morning he stayed up for 50 minutes, taking full advantage of his opportunity.

Tom Sopwith soon realised that Hawker had the makings of a first rate pilot and within a month he had qualified for his Aviator's Certificate which, in those early days, was issued by the Royal Aero Club. His certificate was number 297.

He was placed in charge of the Sopwith's hangars and the competition, demonstration and test flying activities. Considering Hawker had joined Sopwiths at the end of June his rise can be only described as meteoric. At this point he was still only 20 years of age.

About the middle of 1912 it was realised that the facilities at Brooklands were completely inadequate for their rapidly expanding manufacturing activities and Sopwiths bought a disused roller-skating rink at Canbury Park Road, Kingston on Thames, where they started building aeroplanes to their own design. When they were situated at Brooklands the aircraft they built were existing designs such as the Howard Wright.

Kingston was to be the focal point for the production of Sopwith aircraft and subsequently it was used for Hawker aircraft

production, right up to the days of the Hawker Harrier jump jet. Flying operations remained at Brooklands for the time being. Brooklands was one of the earliest, and certainly the most famous, motor-racing track in the world. It was the scene of many exciting races and record runs, with a generous share of spectacular crashes.

Completed in 1907, it had been built by Mr Locke-King, who already owned the land, at a cost of 250,000 pounds, all at his own expense. Plans were drawn up by a Colonel Holden of the Royal Engineers, with the help of a skilled railway engineer Mr Donaldson. They understood the problems involved with the design of such a track and achieved the correct geometry for curves and banking to suit the 120 mph maximum speed envisaged at the time.

Building the track required the services of specialists in earth moving and bridge building. Two thousand workmen were employed and many were housed on the job, first in corrugated iron huts then in more substantial wooden buildings.

The track surface was concrete, 2¾ miles around and 100 feet wide, with banking 30 feet high in places. This track was always a great attraction to Harry because of its flying centre, and had been an important factor in his decision to go to England in 1911.

In the middle of the track there was an open space which, as time went by, was used as a landing ground for the aeroplanes. It followed as a matter of course that people who were interested in motor racing would inevitably be drawn to flying so this activity was welcomed and given every encouragement. Although they did meet with some obstruction from the more conservative Brooklands people.

The concrete track survived until World War II when a part of it was demolished to allow a clear take off for aircraft that were being produced in the Vickers factory situated within the track. The Brooklands Society was formed to restore and maintain those buildings that had survived together with the remaining portion of the track. The old clubhouse and several of the sheds still stand.

Hawker was now taking an increasing role in the development of a team led by Tom Sopwith and Sigrist and was to play an important part in the development of aviation. This was accelerated by the outbreak of World War I.

Chapter Three

Breaking Records

Personal publicity was something Hawker avoided, probably because, like his associates, he was basically a hands-on person who was so intent on getting on with the job that it did not occur to him. As a consequence Hawker was not as widely known, or as well recognised, as he might otherwise have been. The press were not as active then as they are today. Any publicity was a direct result of achievement therefore and was directed to the wonders of this emerging art of building and flying aeroplanes.

The early record attempts were encouraged by generous contributions of prize money. The first of these was made by the Michelin Tyre Company who sponsored the British Empire Michelin Cup. One of the requirements for entries into this competition was that the aircraft had to be of British construction.

During a trip to America Tom Sopwith commissioned a well known boat builder, Burgess, to build under license from Wright Brothers an aeroplane to their design. This aircraft differed from the standard Wright machine in that it was fitted with wing warping type controls with which the whole wing structure was twisted to achieve lateral control, as distinct from the aileron type which is a flap hinged at the outer trailing edge of the wing. It was powered by a Gnome rotary engine and was known as the Burgess Wright biplane. This aeroplane was transported to England where Tom Sopwith replaced the Gnome engine with a British built 40 hp engine.

In order to have an aeroplane which would qualify for entry in the Michelin competition Tom Sopwith manufactured duplicates of all the component parts of the aeroplane in his sheds at Brooklands. The reconstructed aeroplane was therefore of all British construction and satisfied the entry requirements. The machine had twin propellers driven by chains, one of which was crossed to give counter rotation and neutralize the torque of the two propellers. These chains were driven from a single engine which was mounted on the left side of the pilot's seat. A further change to the original design was made to provide some protection from the elements for the pilot in the form of a nacelle, somewhat like a motorcycle sidecar. This was necessary so the pilot could endure the long periods exposed to the elements as record attempts were run over longer and longer times.

This aircraft was then known as the Sopwith-Wright biplane.

Having gained his certificate shortly afterwards Hawker participated in the Quick Starting Competition at Brooklands in the Sopwith Farman aeroplane. Out of the eight entrants he tied for second place with his friend Barnwell. When flying off the dead heat elimination both Hawker and Barnwell flew the course in a faster time than the accredited winner, E.C. Pashley. Tom Sopwith, who competed in two machines, the Sopwith Farman and the Sopwith Tractor, had the doubtful pleasure of being beaten by his pupil.

A few days later, on 15 October 1912, Hawker flew the Burgess Wright for the first time. Although he was accustomed to the Farman type controls he found no difficulty in adapting to the new machine. The following morning he made a test flight of 3 hours 31 minutes in preparation for the British Empire Michelin Cup which carried a prize of 500 pounds.

The Cup had previously been won by Moore-Brabazon in 1909 and twice by Cody in 1910 and 1911. In 1912 a flight of at least five hours had to be completed and the award went to the pilot who remained in the air for the longest time without touching the ground. Apparently entrants were allowed to have several attempts so long as they were completed by 21 October.

Hawker's first attempt ended with a broken valve spring which was a common problem in those days. Following this he made two

(Left) This is believed to be the first aircraft completely designed and built by Sopwiths. It was known as the Tractor biplane and was powered by an 80 hp Gnome engine. Hawker used this aeroplane to establish many records including the altitude records with 1, 2 and 3 passengers.

further attempts. The first, lasting 2 hours 43 minutes, ended with a sudden gale and the second, of 3 hours 28 minutes, ended due to rain. On 24 October he set a record of 8 hours 23 minutes which stood for several years. The same day one other competitor, his friend Raynham who had taken off earlier, held the record for a brief period before being beaten by Hawker. The account of the flight, which appeared in the November issue of the *Aero* magazine, gives a good impression of the day's flying.

"We rose early in the Sopwith camp on Thursday, 24 October. Not that this was the first early morning attempt on the Michelin prize. The same thing had been going on for a week past, and no fewer than three times in this week had the new Sopwith, twin-screw ABC engined biplane sallied forth. Hawker, the pilot, had been chosen to fly the Sopwith, and his determination, skill and enthusiasm through this and the previous attempts justified the faith put in him for such a task. Hawker is a young Australian and, like his fellow countrymen Busteed, Pickles, and Harrison, he shows very great promise as a flier. Joining Sopwith's Flying School as a mechanic he was allowed to learn on the orthodox Farman, and he early displayed his aptitude for this work by going up to 1,000 feet and remaining there for 50 minutes on the fourth day of his training.

"Of his three previous attempts on the Michelin Duration Competition little need be said. The first one was terminated after 3 hours 31 minutes by a valve spring breaking. On the second attempt the wind, after 2 hours 43 minutes, proved too much for further flight. The third attempt ended after 3 hours 28 minutes in a rainstorm, which soaked the magneto through, and temporarily ended its career.

"With serious designs on the duration attempt, the Sopwith camp was awake and bustling, and excitement ran high when it was seen that Raynham was to make a simultaneous attempt on the military Avro biplane (enclosed body type) fitted with a 60 hp Green engine. Hawker got away just before 7 am, but was brought down again after a flight lasting no more than 20 minutes due to intermittent misfiring caused by the magneto cutting out. It was obviously suffering from the effects of its previous soaking. This contingency had been anticipated, however. A brand new British made Bosch had been secured which had arrived late the night before. The old magneto was hurriedly removed and replaced with the new one, but even minor jobs of this kind take time. In this case time was all too precious. When attempting to time the magneto it was found that it had been set to run in the opposite direction to that required. With time fast running out it had to be dismantled and the contact breaker mechanism changed.

"Meanwhile Raynham got away on the Avro at 7.40 am, which gave him a lead of 1 hour 35 minutes by the time Hawker started. Raynham did appear to have trouble in carrying his load as he had to make three attempts before he was able to take off. When he did get off he was flying very carefully through the earlier part of his flight. The Green engine however was running well, with an even beat which seemed to inspire confidence.

"Hawker eventually made a start at 9.15 am. This was the beginning to what would turn out to be a magnificent and exciting contest which lasted until well after dark.

"The ABC spluttered a little at first for want of a warming up, but by the time it had done one circuit of Brooklands its revolutions were up to 2,000 per minute, and Hawker was able to throttle down slightly. There was a tense feeling all round, and an ache in the heart of the Sopwith crew that the magneto had not been properly fitted during the previous night. Hawker's handicap was realised more and more when it was found that if Raynham remained aloft until within 1 hour and 35 minutes of the limiting hours of the competition (which were from sunrise till one hour after sunset), Hawker could not possibly win.

"There was a stream of people to and from the anemometer, which gave the wind speed throughout the day. Happily the wind conditions turned out to be little short of ideal. The speed of the wind during the day did not vary more than 5 to 8 miles per hour.

"Raynham, with his wide experience, took the greatest possible advantage of this, and made a really splendid flight, with the Green engine throttled down to the very slowest revolutions that the machine would maintain height and with the tail dropping in what appeared to be an extreme position to the onlookers.

"Hawker, with tail well up (and his machine lifts the loads remarkably easily) was flying steadily round at a height of about 400 feet, the ABC emitting a steady hum. Raynham, on the other hand, was flying very low and on some occasions was only about 30 feet high. By about 11 am he evidently had become extremely bored with pottering round and round, because he commenced a series of antics round the sheds, and at one time about half way round a turn he suddenly doubled back on his own track and did a turn or two round the wrong way, all the time, however, with his engine ticking round at something like only 950 revolutions per minute, the appearance of the machine being terrifying to behold to those who dread sideslips.

"Hawker all this time was steadily plodding away, making the safest flight possible, and the very machine had a look of determination about it. The two slow speed propellers turned relentlessly. The engine exhaust was a continual buzz because of the high engine speed. That he was out to win if possible was obvious from every movement. Raynham's champions grew a little nervous over the flippancy of their pilot, and a shutter of one of the sheds was quickly requisitioned on which were painted the words in large letters, 'Fly Higher'. It had not much effect, however, although it served apparently to sober him a little.

"Towards 1 pm impatient questions as to how much oil and petrol they were carrying began to circulate amongst the onlookers. It appeared that Raynham's oil supply was likely to run out before anything else. On more than one occasion the Green suddenly slowed down in revolutions, only to pick up again just as quickly. Someone pointed out later on that the short pipes coupled to the exhaust ports in the cylinders of the Green no longer emitted the puffs of smoke that had been prominent in the earlier stages of the flight, and misgivings that the oil supply would give out began to circulate.

"Excitement reached fever heat between 2 and 3 pm. The strain of watching the two machines circle round hour after hour becoming intense. It was not even like a motor race, where one can often see, fairly early, who is likely to be the winner. In this competition speed did not even count, and the contest might terminate any second by either running out of fuel or by an engine failure. Little work was done in the sheds, and every few minutes mechanics would appear at the various doors to find and call out to their mates that both machines were still up.

" 'Raynham's down!' The cry spread across the ground at about 3.10 pm. A frantic rush was made to the front of the sheds and, sure enough, he was just on the point of touching down. He terminated his

Cochrane House
Newfoundland
April 15ᵗʰ 1919

Dear Dad

Just a few lines to let you know
things are going over here. I suppose you all by the
papers that I am over here now waiting to have a
go at flying the Atlantic. Well we are now standing
round waiting for weather and may get off any day
now. We have another machine called the Martinsyde
that is to be flown by Raynham they are all ready to
go it just means which one gets off first now, that
means keeping a good watch on one another and a good
watch on the weather too, but I hope to be off this week at
any rate. There is not much news to tell you here
only I have been very busy with this job for the
last 3 months. I suppose you will get all the news in
the papers about the flight quicker than I can get
it to you by post.

Every one is quite well at home as I hope they are
keeping out there. I will send you a cable when
I get to England or Ireland so you will know everything
is alright. The papers are all full of the Atlantic
flight here and any little of what they talk about
is right but it fills up the paper
Well must close now love to all at home
from your loving Son
Harry

This photo of Harry Hawker appeared as the frontispiece in the book Muriel wrote about her husband.

(Left) A facsimile copy of a letter written by Harry to his father in Australia, which comments on his forthcoming Atlantic attempt.

flight at 3.11 pm exactly, having been in the air 7 hours 31 minutes, truly a splendid performance. We all rushed across the ground, and Fred May, of the Green Engine Company, jumped into his car and came tearing up to the spot. Raynham climbed out, looking somewhat tired, but apparently none the worse for his time in the air. He said that the oil had run out and, though he had held on as long as he could, the engine had been dropping in revolutions for the last half hour, and he did not want to risk it seizing up altogether.

"Up to the very minute of Raynham's landing it is doubtful if a single person on Brooklands would have given a shilling for Hawker's chance of putting up a better time than Raynham with the latter's hour and a half start. The situation had now changed dramatically as all eyes were turned upwards, ears listening for any change in the rhythmic beat of the engine. The question went round, 'Will he keep up for another two hours?' The engine sounded happy enough, and if nothing happened there was no reason why he should not, as he had a big load of fuel. The excitement now began steadily to rise as the minutes were ticked off, to the Sopwith enthusiasts, every minute seemed an age. They all went back to find something to do that would pass the time more quickly, but had to come out again with dread in their hearts that they might find Hawker taxiing along the ground.

"Gradually the time passed. Hawker was still steadily flying at his 400 feet altitude. Then Tom Sopwith appeared on the scene at about 4 pm, and brought out his 70 hp Gnome Tractor biplane with the intention of cheering Hawker up a little. Taking Charteris as a passenger, he did one or two circuits, climbing up to Hawker's level then, very skilfully, cut across a sharp turn and came alongside. Hawker, in fear of not lasting out the time, had throttled down to the minimum at which he could maintain height so as to economize petrol and oil. His machine was therefore flying very slowly. Tom Sopwith had to throttle right back so as not to pass him. The two on the Tractor waved frantically, and shouted encouragements, which, of course, Hawker could not hear at all, but which he undoubtedly understood. Down planed the Tractor again, leaving Hawker with just another half hour to go through to equal Raynham's time, a record which, by the way, was only to stand for 1 hour 35 minutes as the British Duration Record.

"The next half hour was the most anxious period experienced by a great number of the Brooklands clan. It is doubtful if any other event ever held on the ground has caused so much interest. Tea was forgotten altogether, and exact minutes and seconds were in the greatest demand, everybody walking about watch in hand. After 10 minutes had passed it was observed that Hawker had throttled really to the very limit so as not to run the slightest risk of running short of petrol. The machine was flying at a terrible angle, with the tail pointing strongly earthwards. The spectators began to feel nervous. Another shutter was acquired, on which was whitewashed, 'Keep your tail up'. This was displayed for the pilot who, however, took but little notice of it.

"Gradually the minutes passed. A small crowd gathered round the timekeeper, who slowly (horribly slowly to some) counted 9 minutes, 8 minutes, and so on. 'One more circuit will do it!' someone cried, and it did, and as the last seconds passed away, never to be recalled, a huge sigh escaped from everyone there. To some it was a sigh of relief, to others perhaps not, but now the crisis was over everybody was sporting enough to express admiration for a very plucky flight.

"Hawker had evidently had his eye glued to the clock which he carried on board, for now he had raised the tail again, and the machine sped away full of life. The time also slipped by much faster now that the face of the watch was not being scrutinized so carefully. Another half hour passed when darkness began to close in. It had been arranged that a huge petrol fire should be lit when it was time for Hawker to come down, an hour after sunset being 5.48 pm. It was, however, quite dark at 5.20 pm, and a difficult problem arose in the minds of those on the ground. It was naturally wished to make the flight as long as possible, and therefore to light the bonfire then would have been to bring him down unnecessarily early, on the other hand, complete darkness might quite possibly cause him to lose himself. A better arrangement would have been to light one fire half an hour before the specified finish, another one a quarter of an hour later, and a third when the time was up, leaving the whole three for him to land by.

"Any misgivings that may have remained in the minds of a few regarding the condition of the engine were quickly put at rest by Hawker, at about 5.30 pm, opening the throttle wide and shooting up to between 1,200 and 1,500 feet in so short a space of time as would have made some of our military competitors envious. It was evident he did this to run no risk of petrol running out when he was over the sewage farm or behind the sheds at a low altitude. It was now quite dark, and wanted but 10 minutes to the time limit. At this stage everyone was impressed by the appearance of the long flame from the exhaust. The exhaust pipes were apparently quite red-hot the whole time.

"Suddenly Hawker was seen to be intent on making a landing without further delay. He came down in a perfectly straight line from the far end of the ground with the engine about half throttled. He made a very shallow angle of descent, apparently with the intention of striking as gradually as possible, as the earth could not be seen at all. Those in charge of the bonfires instantly realised the situation, and applied matches to the petrol, which flared up in the nick of time. Hawker straightened up, closed the throttle, and made a perfect landing 7 minutes before the time limit.

"There was a rush for the spot where the machine had landed. The next 5 minutes were occupied in cheering, congratulations, shaking hands and patting backs. Hawker climbed out of his seat, having been exactly 8 hours 23 minutes in the air, but he looked easily capable of undergoing the same trial again."

Hawker later went on to relate this record breaking experience as follows:

"When I got away first at about 9.15 am I thought the new magneto had been timed incorrectly, because the engine was only turning at 1,600 rpm and barely produced enough power to fly the aeroplane with its heavy load of fuel. Before I had done a circuit, however, I discovered it was only a case of getting the engine warm. This was taking a particularly long time, because we had fitted two radiators. When the engine warmed up properly it ran along steadily at about 1,800 rpm.

"I was extremely worried to think that we had let Raynham get such a lead, but there was no help for it now, so I settled down to a long, slow job, determined to stick it out to the end.

"I was quite snug and warm inside the little body that had been provided. The weather throughout was ideal. The engine continued to run splendidly, and I can truthfully say that it never made a single misfire for the whole period of 8 hours 23 minutes.

I occupied most of my time in keeping one eye on the clock and one on Raynham, who was flying below me. On several occasions he appeared to be so low that he appeared to be taxiing along the ground. I always noticed that he never came to rest, however, and concluded that he must be flying low. Once he shot across my path about some 150 feet under me, giving me quite a start for the second. On several occasions I lost sight of him for half an hour at a time, and was sometimes worried by wondering whether I was going to give him my back wash or whether I was getting into his.

"I had a Thermos flask of cocoa on board, some chocolate, and some sandwiches, all of which I found useful in either passing the time away or relieving the monotony by giving me something to do. I did not look at the exact time that I started, but I knew that I had about an hour and three quarters to do after Raynham had finished. Everything was plain sailing with regard to the petrol supply and oil. The petrol was gravity fed and the oil pressure fed. I had a 20 gallon petrol tank just behind my back, which was coupled directly to the carburettor. Above that I had a 12 gallon tank which was connected to the larger tank by a pipe. After I had been flying for 4 hours I turned on the tap from the 12 gallon tank which allowed the contents to flow down to replenish the larger main tank. I discovered afterwards that the pipe between the two tanks was not large enough, because when I came down in the evening I could hear the petrol still slowly trickling into the large tank. For the oil, I had a glass gauge on the sump of the motor. A 5 gallon oil tank, with a tap between the tank and the sump allowed me to replenish the oil level in the sump when it was required. As the petrol was used and the weight decreased I was able to close the throttle slightly. The engine was still running well at all speeds.

"Later on I saw a shutter being carried out with the words 'Fly Higher' painted on it. I could read it quite distinctly from 400 feet, but as I felt quite comfortable where I was I did not pay any heed to it. It was not until after I came down that I discovered that this sign was meant for Raynham. It was a great relief to me to see Raynham come down, and I knew this time that he was going to land, because I could see all the people running across the ground towards him.

"From then onwards I kept my eyes glued to the face of the clock, the last half hour that would make my flight equal Raynham's being the most anxious and worrying of the whole day. Every minute seemed an hour. As I was afraid that the petrol in the top tank might not be flowing properly into the main tank, I closed the throttle for the last 20 minutes down to the very limit the machine would fly with, to allow the petrol time to run down to the lower tank. I must have been then flying at only about 35 miles per hour. Then I saw the 70 hp Gnome Tractor bus come out and watched Tom Sopwith with interest. I guessed what he was coming out for, and when I saw him make straight for me. I kept on a perfectly straight course, knowing well that he would be careful not to hinder me in any way. He came quite close alongside, and I distinctly heard them both shout (my ABC engine had a silencer fitted) but I could not tell what they said. Painfully slowly the minutes rolled away, but at last I realised that I was the holder of the British Duration Record. When I was quite sure of this I opened up the throttle again, as I had not much to fear now. However, I was still determined to keep in the air for as long as possible in order to give anyone else a good run in order to beat it. When it was getting nearly dark I pulled open the last notch of the throttle and climbed up to 1,400 feet on the altimeter, and I did this very rapidly as my fuel load by this time was very low. Darkness came on. I could see very little but the red-hot exhaust pipe and the reflection from the burnt gases. The dim lights of the Blue Bird served as a little guide to the position of the ground, and when I felt sure it must be quite 5.50 pm I decided to come down immediately and make a guess at where the ground was, as I felt sure they had forgotten all about the fires. I did not want to get lost and smash the machine up. Just as I was landing however the fires flared up, and I came to rest safely. Everyone as pleased as I was that I had been successful in securing the record."

Hawker's success in winning both the British Empire Michelin Cup and also the British Endurance Record established him immediately

18c AUSTRALIA

HARRY HAWKER

(Upper left) *The stamp, overprinted for an April attempt which never took place, which was used on both Hawker's salvaged mail and Alcock's actual crossing.*

(Lower left) *Alcock and Brown successfully flew the Atlantic some two weeks after Hawker's attempt. They all signed this commemoration card for the Newfoundland Disaster Fund.*

(Upper) *In 1985 the Australian Postal Authorities issued five "Famous Aviator" stamps. Hawker was on the 18c denomination.*

(Right) *The salvaged mail from the Atlantic is now much prized by collectors. This cutting is from the* Daily Mail *dated 1970.*

FAR & NEAR

£1,650 for an old envelope

A SEA-STAINED envelope, addressed to the 'Right Hon. Viscount Northcliffe,' was sold for £1,650 in London yesterday.

The envelope was in the Sopwith plane piloted by Harry Hawker which crashed in the Daily Mail £10,000 Transatlantic competition in 1919. He was rescued, the plane and mailbag were salvaged and the letters were all delivered.

The Northcliffe letter, bearing a three cent Newfoundland brown stamp, was bought by a private buyer yesterday in the Stanley Gibbons saleroom. It was sold as part of the Sidney Harris Newfoundland Collection.

in the front rank of British pilots. Public attention was drawn to the newly formed Sopwiths at a time when it was needed. The company was taking advantage of every opportunity to promote flying in general, and Sopwiths aeroplanes in particular, as a market had to be created if the company was going to survive.

Various flying events were organized which were attended by vast crowds who flocked to see this thrilling new sport. It did not take long however for people to become aware of the potential uses for the aeroplane in commercial and military fields. The keen competition between the aircraft builders and pilots was to play an important part in aeroplane development. These flying events were mainly held at Brooklands but as time went by more and more activities took place at Hendon Airfield, near London, which was flat and open, with no conflicting racetrack.

On 9 November an Altitude Competition was held in which the only two entrants were Barnwell and Hawker. The former won this because Hawker's barograph was not set correctly prior to take off.

On 16 November a Bomb Dropping and Landing Competition was held. In this competitors were required to drop dummy bombs on a target and then land within a given radius of a target. There were six entrants but this time Hawker was unsuccessful. Tom Sopwith made a direct hit with his bomb but misjudged his landing, which put him out of contention.

The following day, 17 November, the weather was perfect and Hawker was more successful in the Relay, or Despatch Carrying, Race. In this contest the pilots worked in pairs. One would take off with the despatch and after flying one and a half laps of a designated course land, hand them over to the other pilot who would take-off in another aeroplane and fly a further one and a half laps, land and hand the despatch to the Judge. It was originally intended that each pair should comprise a biplane and a monoplane. One pilot, Hamel, flew over from Hendon in a Bleriot for the event. The scarcity of monoplanes was due to a ban, for some obscure reason, on monoplanes by the War Office, resulting in only biplanes taking part. First Prize went to Hawker flying a Sopwith aeroplane, and Spencer who flew an aircraft of his own construction. Their total time for the event was 9 minutes 30 seconds. Barnwell and Merriam flying Farman and Bristol machines respectively, took 10 minutes 10 seconds and Bendall and Knight took 10 minutes 12 seconds, so the competition was very strong.

Just before dusk on 24 November a Speed Handicap contest was run over two laps of the Brooklands course. The handicapping was well worked out as the first three competitors home, Alcock, Sopwith and Knight finished in that order within the space of a few seconds. Hawker was unplaced.

The three Australian friends who had come to England had now achieved notable success in the aviation world. Busteed and Harrison were well known and successful as flying instructors. Hawker was carrying out record-making flights and establishing his position in the Sopwith organisation, which was rapidly expanding.

The latter half of 1912 had been very successful for Hawker as he had achieved so much. His decision to go to England was, at last, turning out to be a good one. He could now reasonably expect his career to go forward in this new and exciting industry which was showing such promise. Little were they to know that in a couple of short years their skills and knowledge were to be put to much more serious use with the outbreak of World War I.

The Sopwith Batboat just before leaving the water on take-off. Note the retracted wheels. This was the first true amphibian aeroplane.

The Batboat with its wheels down and about to land on a field close to the sea.

Chapter Four

Racing

During the early part of 1913 Hawker carried out many flying demonstrations and competed for a number of prizes.

One of the chief benefactors of aviation at the time, Lord Northcliffe, owned the *Daily Mail* newspaper. It was his generous provision of prize money and financial support that contributed much to this new, and rapidly growing, means of transport.

It was becoming apparent that flying could have practical applications in travel, commerce and warfare, as distinct from the adventurous activity indulged in by a few eccentrics — as some regarded these early aviators.

Aviation was really on the move as an industry. The aviation companies, although not prospering, were building up their potential in order to take advantage of what they could see would be the certain commercial development of the aeroplane. Hawker was right in the middle of this activity being involved both as a test pilot and a designer with Sopwiths. These were practical people caught up in the enthusiasm of a burgeoning industry.

Sir Charles Rose Bt MP, Chairman of the Royal Aero Club, on 7 January 1913, handed Hawker, representing Sopwiths, a cheque for 500 pounds, the prize for winning the Michelin Duration Record Competition.Of this Hawker received 25% in recognition of his special services to Sopwiths.

On 7 February Hawker, with Tom Sopwith piloting, tested the new Sopwith biplane which more than lived up to expectations. This was the first wholly Sopwith designed and built aeroplane, a three-seater known as a Tractor. It had three celluloid windows on each side in the fuselage and there was room for two passengers, who were seated in front of the pilot. It was powered by an 80 hp Gnome rotary engine.

The prototype was sent to Olympia for the Aero Show where it was purchased by the Admiralty. This was subsequently followed by a further order for three more planes.

Also on show was the Sopwith Batboat. This was a biplane on a boat fuselage powered by a six cylinder, water-cooled engine mounted between the wings. Testing began on 7 March but it did not perform very well and was unfortunately destroyed by a gale at its moorings.

A later version was built with a 100 hp engine which improved the performance. Other improvements were made including fitting ailerons in place of wing-warping for lateral control.

The building of the Batboats probably stemmed from Tom Sopwith's great interest in boats and yachts. He was a prominent competitor in the America's Cup which, in recent years, has become the world's premier yacht race. Sopwith's interest in aeroplanes built to take off from water continued over the years, with a number of seaplanes being designed, notably one for the Round Britain Race and for the Schneider Trophy Races.

Hawker took part in a number of flying events over the early part of 1913. On 31 May, together with some other well known pilots, it was decided that an attempt would be made on the British and possibly the World Altitude Record, under the supervision of the Royal Aero Club. One pilot, Hamel, would fly an 80 hp Borel monoplane, Gordon Bell the 120 hp Martin-Handasyde monoplane, and Hawker the 80 hp Gnome Sopwith Tractor biplane. The Brooklands Automobile Racing Club offered a prize of 50 pounds to anyone breaking the existing record of 10,650 feet which was held by Geoffrey de Havilland. The following extract has been taken from the official notice of the Royal Aero Club dated 7 June 1913.

"British Altitude Record: The report of the flight made by Mr H.G. Hawker at Brooklands on 31 May 1913, together with barograph charts, were considered, and it was decided to accept the height reached, 11,450 feet, as a British height record. The aircraft used on the occasion was a Sopwith Tractor biplane, fitted with an 80 hp Gnome engine."

Sopwiths were now becoming established and sold the Admiralty three Tractor land planes which had proved so successful. These were fitted with 100 hp Gnome engines. The army was now displaying interest in the original land plane version of the Tractor.

By this time aileron control had replaced wing-warping as the standard form of lateral control. Hawker's experience in flying and involvement in design ensured that he was, to a large extent, responsible for this change.

In the early days, some method was required to control an aeroplane on its rolling axis. Wing-warping seemed to be the simplest solution.

The main structural members of the wings were the front spar and a rear spar which extended for the length of the wing. The wing ribs which had the aerofoil profile necessary to provide the lift were fixed at right angles to the spars, these in turn supported, and gave shape to, the fabric covering.

Bracing wires and struts, between the upper and lower wings in the case of the biplane, provided the structure with the required strength to support the aeroplane and its load. In a monoplane the bracing

The Great Flight

Route and Controls

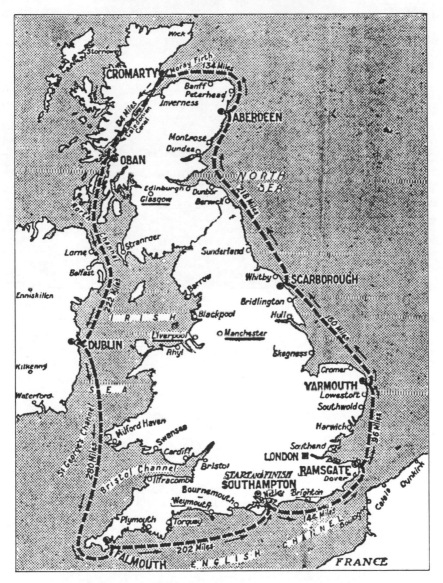

This old map, taken from a contemporary newspaper, shows the
route that the organizers planned for the Round Britain Air
Race. Hawker crashed some 15 miles short of Dublin.

(Upper left) A Tractor aeroplane, adapted by the addition of floats, was entered in the Round Britain Race. Kauper is on the left and Hawker on the right. Note the crowds lining the foreshore.

(Lower left) An interesting picture showing how the plane almost sank at Oban, Scotland, because the floats became waterlogged.

(Upper) The Tractor taking off. Note the tail float keeping the rudder clear of the water.

*The Tractor being waved off on one of the legs. Flying events were beginning
to generate a great deal of interest from the general public.*

wires went to the kingpost on top of the fuselage and to the undercarriage below.

The bracing to the front spar was fixed in the wing-warping control system. The wires that went to the attachment points on the rear spar, however, were connected by a system of pulleys and levers to the control stick. This enabled the pilot to control the angle of incidence of the outer part of the wing and, consequently, the angle at which this part of the wing met the airflow. The lift was correspondingly increased, or decreased, giving control in the rolling plane.

A serious flaw inherent to this system was thought to have caused a great number of accidents. The problem was when the control warped the wing, to raise the wing on that side, it took the angle of attack (which is the angle the wing meets the air) above the critical angle of about 14 degrees. The wing consequently suffered an aerodynamic stall and fell very suddenly without warning, which was the very opposite to what was intended. This resulted in a sideslip, or a spin, often with disastrous results. This frequently occurred close to the ground when there was insufficient height for a recovery to be made.

The solution to the problem was to brace the rear spar to a fixed position. The wing as a whole then became a relatively solid structure. A section at the outer end of the wing, back from the rear spar, was then removed and replaced with a hinged flap, known as an aileron, which was under the control of the pilot through his control stick. This enabled one side to go up and the other down. This gave the desired control without changing the angle of incidence of the wing structure.

Mr Mortimer Singer, of Singer sewing machine fame, put up prize money for the first pilot to complete a course on the Solent (a strait of the English Channel between the south coast of England and the Isle of Wight). The conditions were that six return flights had to be made on the course from a point on the land to a point at sea, not less than 5 miles distant in a direct line. The latter point was to be not less than 1 mile from any shore. Landings had to be made on arrival at each point. The time allowed to complete the course was 5 hours. After several attempts Hawker, flying the Sopwith Batboat, was finally successful in completing the course on 8 July in a time of 3 hours 25 minutes.

The Royal Aero Club announced a prize, again donated by the *Daily Mail*, of 5,000 pounds for a Circuit of Great Britain. The final list of entries closed on 1 August with four entrants, Sopwith, Cody, Radley and McClean. Hawker and Kauper were to fly the Sopwith entry but the other entrants dropped out, leaving them as the sole competitors. Tragically, Cody had been killed in a crash just a few days before and the others had recurring engine troubles which prevented them from taking part.

The competition was to start on 16 August. Competitors were required to fly over a circuit of 1,540 miles, within 72 consecutive hours, starting from Southampton Water and tracking via Ramsgate, Yarmouth, Scarborough, Aberdeen, Oban, Dublin, Falmouth to finish at Southampton Water. They were required to land in specified areas at sea for identification by officials of the Royal Aero Club.

The aircraft therefore were, of necessity, seaplanes. The rules of the competition allowed the attempt to be made in any 72 consecutive hour period up to 30 August. No flying was allowed on Sunday, so that it was possible for them to fly on Saturday, rest on Sunday, and complete the course on Monday and Tuesday. This allowed minor repairs, or adjustments, to be carried out. Major parts of the engine and aircraft were sealed by the Royal Aero Club to make sure no major changes of equipment were carried out. One passenger was required to be carried and Hawker was accompanied by his old friend Kauper. Each competitor carried a time card which had to be signed by an official of the Royal Aero Club at each control point.

The public showed enormous interest in this competition because of the tremendous challenge it presented the crew and the aircraft. Views were expressed that it was impossible to complete the course in the allotted time.

Hawker and Kauper finally departed from the Solent on 16 August in the Sopwith seaplane which was a development of the three-seater. They tracked for Ramsgate and Yarmouth where Hawker was taken ill, probably due to inhaling fumes from the exhaust system of the engine. They spent the night there and, although Hawker had recovered by the morning, the weather deteriorated to such an extent that there was no alternative but to abandon the attempt. They seized the opportunity to have the exhaust system improved by lengthening the pipe to keep the fumes clear of the cockpit.

The Royal Aero Club declared the event "no contest" under the circumstances and fixed another starting date, 25 August, with the hope that another competitor might show up to challenge Hawker and Kauper and stimulate more public interest. Once again they were the only starters. The flight went reasonably well until just before Dublin when Hawker was forced to land to make some minor adjustments to the engine. On the approach the aircraft sideslipped into the water. Hawker was not hurt but Kauper suffered a broken arm.

Hawker's version of the cause of the accident was that, with no end stops fitted to the rudder bar, his foot slipped off the end causing the loss of control at such a critical time. They had covered 1,043 miles in two and a half days, which was a very creditable performance, and the *Daily Mail*, very sportingly, gave Hawker 1,000 pounds for his gallant effort.

Hawker was prepared to accept the blame rather than have any doubts cast on the aeroplane or the engine. He almost certainly had a problem that gave him no choice but to land within 15 miles of Dublin. The engine had been plagued with valve spring breakages and a mechanic from the factory had brought a full set of valves and cages over to Dublin to replace the ones which had been giving trouble. Had they been able to make that last 15 miles, and have these replacements fitted, they would undoubtedly have been able to complete the course.

Aeroplane engines were in very short supply at this time so the engine was salvaged and, after being completely overhauled, was fitted into the latest Tractor biplane from the works.

Hawker test flew the machine on 4 October 1913, after which a few necessary adjustments were made. Four days later he took off from the grass in front of the Sopwith's sheds at Brooklands and set off in the direction of Cobham. As he rose over the trees bordering the Weybridge-Byfleet road a down current caught the aeroplane. Realising that a crash was inevitable Hawker took his feet off the rudder bar and braced himself. The machine hit the ground in a sideslip so that the crumpling wing absorbed the main force of impact. Apart from straining a back muscle and bruising his forehead he escaped injury. Again he accepted the blame for the crash which he put down to carelessness.

A strong breeze had been blowing at the time and he was not able to gain a safe margin of height over the trees before striking the turbulence they generated.

Reports of this accident from other sources indicate that this was a much more violent crash than related above and that he was in hospital for a short time after. It was also thought to be the origin of the serious back trouble which was to plague him for the rest of his life.

Hawker took part in a considerable number of flying competitions during the year. By doing this he was building up a great wealth of experience in aeroplane performance, leading to increased knowledge of what was required in their construction. Throughout the week he was working long hours in the factory with Tom Sopwith and Sigrist, designing and supervising the building of new and improved types of aeroplanes.

The fruits of all this emerged at the end of 1913 with the appearance of the Sopwith Tabloid, which was a considerable improvement on anything that had been built before. It was a small side by side two-seater biplane, powered by an 80 hp Gnome rotary engine, with a top speed of 90 mph. The wing span was 26 feet and the overall length 25 feet. The prototype Tabloid, with a wheeled undercarriage, arrived

at Brooklands on 27 November where it was immediately rigged and successfully test flown by Hawker. The plane was very docile to handle and he was delighted with its qualities. It was to be the forerunner of the single-seater fighters that followed during the course of World War I. This machine was the one which accompanied him to Australia.

The Tabloid was put into production at Kingston on Thames together with two variants, a single-seater version which became known as the Sopwith Schneider, and the Sopwith Baby.

The Tabloid was such a success that Tom Sopwith entered one fitted with a 100 hp Monosoupape Gnome engine in the Schneider Trophy race which was due to take place at Monaco on 20 April 1914. Howard Pixton, who had taken over Hawker's role while he was away in Australia, was to be the pilot. There were some early problems as the first conversion from a landplane to a seaplane, which was required under the rules of the contest, was not very successful. It was fitted with a single float but failed to leave the water at Hamble during trials there on 1 April. In fact the aeroplane somersaulted and Pixton was thrown into the water.

During the next 19 days the aeroplane was rebuilt and fitted with a twin-float undercarriage and an additional fuel tank to give it the required range of 2 hours. It was also fitted with a coarser pitch propellor, to reduce the engine rpm, and was taxied on the Thames before being crated at Kingston. From there it was sent to Monaco, where it arrived in time to be at the starting line at 8.00 am on 20 April.

Pixton completed 28 laps (175 miles) over the stipulated course in 2 hours 13 seconds, averaging 85.5 mph, thereby winning the Schneider Trophy. Instead of landing immediately, Pixton flew flat out for an additional two laps and thus achieved a world speed record with a total 187 miles at an average speed of 92 mph. The Sopwith team had beaten the French, Swiss and the one other British entrant, by a wide margin. This victory gained Sopwiths international prestige and had far reaching results.

(Upper left) The last straw! The wreckage from the crash near Dublin that put an end to Hawker's hopes of completing the Round Britain Race.

(Lower left) The damaged floats after they had been salvaged.

The Tabloid, assembled in Australia, on the golf course at Elsternwick. In the foreground, Harry's father, George, stands proudly next to the aeroplane.

Chapter Five

Australia

Harry Hawker and his friend Kauper arrived in Melbourne on the RMS *Maloja* on 19 January 1914.

In the hold of the ship was the Tabloid aeroplane which they had brought out to give demonstrations aimed at popularising aviation in Australia, and to try and impress upon commercial interests, politicians and the military forces the part that they envisaged aeroplanes could play in the future or in any war.

They would also be able to spend some time with their families and friends, after being away from them for three years. Hawker's exploits in England, where he had built up a fine reputation, had been widely reported in the Australian press so he arrived in Australia as something of a hero and in an atmosphere of "local boy makes good". Great crowds turned out whenever he carried out flying demonstrations.

A civic reception had been arranged at the St Kilda Town Hall shortly after his arrival and a distinguished assembly gathered to honour Hawker. The presence of the Postmaster General gives some idea of the significance of the occasion, as the postal authorities had still to be convinced of the value of using aircraft to carry mail. The Mayor said in his address that they had all followed with the greatest interest one of their local boy's achievements in the old country, and that they hoped on his return he would establish further records in the world of flight.

Another speaker pointed out that it was only by the push and energy of their young citizens at the other end of the world that Australia had any recognition overseas. He expressed regret that Hawker had to leave Australia again, but hoped that when he returned they would be able to congratulate him on still greater achievements.

Harry's father said that amidst all the successes and applause his son had not forgotten his home. He had brought an aeroplane, partly of his own design, with him. It was so new that it had not, at that time, been publicly demonstrated in England. The people of Melbourne were to have the first opportunity to see the very latest aeroplane fly.

Hawker responded to the speeches by expressing his pleasure that, as an Australian, he had achieved his successes in England and, on his return, he would do his best on behalf of Australia.

In an interview with the press he said that the difference between a modern biplane, such as he had with him, and the old Bristol Boxkite biplane (an example of which the Australian Government had acquired) was as great as between a motor car and a bullock waggon. Aviation had made great strides in the last year or two. The Boxkite biplanes were still considered as serviceable school machines, but did not have sufficient speed for military requirements, which the higher powered, modern machines undoubtedly possessed. The cost of the Tabloid and the Boxkite machine were about the same and, considering its power, the former was the cheapest machine on the market at that time.

There is no doubt that in visiting his native land Hawker was on a sales mission on behalf of Sopwiths. He took every opportunity to promote aviation in general and the very latest Sopwith aeroplanes in particular.

During one interview Hawker spoke of the natural stability that is built into an aeroplane. He considered the common fear that one could turn upside down was quite unfounded, and went on to say:

"Flying is full of interest and not half so difficult as the public imagines. Over ninety percent of accidents are due to carelessness, not necessarily on the part of the pilot, but of workmen who leave wires slack and do not check the structural parts of the aeroplane."

Hawker was well and truly aware of the need to check and double check everything before taking an aeroplane into the air. Some of the accounts of his flights in England would lead one to believe that he was inclined to take too much for granted, but this was not correct. Reports from press clippings in Australia emphasized the meticulous care with which he carried out preflight inspections - this was the only way he survived. He was an experienced mechanic and very conscious of safety.

There is no doubt that he had led a charmed life when one considers all the test flying that he carried out. One thing that does stand out was his intense loyalty to the firm he was representing. There are numerous incidents where he accepted the blame for some mishap when it was very doubtful that he was at fault.

No time was lost in assembling the Tabloid which was done at the C.L.C. Garage and Engineering Works at Melbourne. This was a partnership of Chamberlain, Lawrence and Clendinnon who had the agency for Crossley motor cars. A.W. Chamberlain was Hawker's brother-in-law, having married his elder sister, Maude. C.L.C. was, therefore, a natural base for operations, particularly as it was adjacent to New Street and Elsternwick Golf Course, from which Hawker could take off and land. The initial flights were delayed because the special castor oil for lubricating the Gnome engine was held up in customs. His first flight was therefore not until 27 January.

There is an account of Hawker's preflight inspection and it indicates that a very thorough inspection was carried out on this occasion. A paragraph from one press report is worth quoting. It seems that some of the pilots who had previously given flying demonstrations in Australia were showmen and Hawker's performance represented a much more responsible and businesslike approach, such as one would expect from a professional airman.

"There was nothing theatrical about the preparations. The hero of the day did not gaze anxiously aloft, frown and shake his head. He did not have long and heated arguments with his mechanic, nor did he attire himself in large yellow clothes or look unduly nonchalant with a cigarette hanging from the lower lip. The onlookers, contrary perhaps to expectations, saw only a man whose interest was centred in practical preparations for the flight."

When the special oil was finally cleared through customs and delivered, the aeroplane was wheeled out of the garage and final preparations were made for its initial Australian flight. It is almost impossible to imagine, looking at New Street as it is now, that such an event could have taken place there.

Hawker took his seat in the cockpit, the propeller was swung, and the engine burst into life sending hats flying and raising considerable dust. Having run the engine up and satisfied himself that all was in order, he waved his arm and the four dust covered helpers, who had been holding the machine, let go. The aeroplane took off down New Street with crowds lining the footpaths on each side. After a short run it rose into the air and climbed steeply, turning west over the golf course. The crowd responded with a mighty cheer. A horse, drawing a van, was badly frightened, reared up and took some time to pacify, adding more excitement to the occasion.

At a height of about 600 feet Hawker did some right and left-hand turns, banked at an angle of 45 degrees or more, dived to within a few feet of the ground at unprecedented speed and then proceeded to hedgehop over trees and fences. He then climbed higher and set off towards Toorak at about 5,000 feet and then turned to fly down the Yarra River. He glided down above the grounds of Government House and then opened the engine up at 2,000 feet, crossed above Albert Park over the lake, and returned to the golf course, where he landed. He had been in the air about 20 minutes.

His return was greeted by much cheering, but he made sure his aeroplane was safely back in the garage before responding to calls for speeches and interviews. He commented that the air was so much clearer than it was in England that he could see Geelong and to see such a distance would not have been possible in the atmosphere over there. He reported that everything worked perfectly, that he had reached a height of 5,000 feet and was flying at 90 mph.

He explained a point that needed emphasizing to the Australian crowds, and that was that it was extremely dangerous to get in the way of an aeroplane when it was taking off or landing, because of the propeller. There had been very serious accidents at flying meetings when people had crowded in too close and were struck by the propeller.

This short trial flight made quite an impact on the crowd. As one report said, "...the value of swift flight under precise control in warfare was appreciated by the onlookers as of incalculable value."

On the afternoon of 3 February the Governor, Lord Denman, received a telephone call saying Hawker had just left Elsternwick and was on his way over. Lord Denman and his wife and some friends, who were about to play tennis, barely had time to reach the lawn before he arrived at about 3,000 feet.

"...as soon as he was above his destination he began to descend in a magnificent spiral, round and round at a terrific speed. As he came nearer to the ground he executed several manoeuvres for the benefit of those below. Making sharp turns he banked his machine to such a degree that many considered it miraculous that he kept his seat at all. Then, when above the polo ground and facing Government House, he glided down to a perfect landing."

Hawker's main concern while flying over was thinking how he should present himself to the Governor. As the Tabloid came to rest, Lord Denman and his party walked over to find an unassuming, clean shaven, young man dressed in a lounge suit and tie, wearing a cap, clean and unruffled as if he had done no more than walk in off the road outside. Nervously Hawker shook hands with the Governor and the rest of the party. Aeroplanes and flying were the subject of conversation for the half an hour that he stayed, during which Hawker explained features of the aircraft.

Lord Denman was very interested in aviation. Before leaving England he had flown as a passenger in a Grahame-White aeroplane. The Governor's aide, Capt Pollocks, had also had some flying experience in England. The departure from Government House was as informal as the arrival and after thanking Lord Denman for his warm reception, Hawker started the engine and took off. He then put on a bit of a show for the benefit of the Governor and his party and returned to Elsternwick where he again gave a spirited display of flying before landing on the golf links.

After landing he took some old friends for flights and was approached by two young ladies who wished to make flights. This was arranged for the following Saturday although one of them, Miss Dixon, offered 10 pounds to be taken up straight away so that she might have the distinction of being the first lady passenger in Australia.

The newspapers, reporting the day's activities, advised that Hawker would be flying the following Saturday at Caulfield racecourse. He planned to make six flights altogether, on four of which he would carry passengers at 20 pounds each. Anticipating large crowds, the Tourist Bureau had on sale combined rail and admission tickets. Arrangements were made to handle the expected crowds and special services were run on the railway and trams to cope with the crowds.

In the meantime there were objections to the use of the racecourse for this purpose and letters were written to the papers on the subject. However the display went on and a crowd of 20,000 to 30,000 people turned up. Hawker had captured the imagination of the public. Eighteen special trains were run from Flinders Street and the roads to the racecourse were choked. Unfortunately the crowd was too great for the authorities and the police to handle, and people invaded the racecourse straight which had been selected for take off and landing. After making two flights the crowd had become so unmanageable that Hawker decided it was too dangerous to continue flying from there.

He took Miss Dixon, with whom he had made the arrangement the previous Saturday, for the return flight to Elsternwick. However a crowd had gathered there also and made a safe landing difficult. He ran out of grass strip while trying to avoid people and the aeroplane was slightly damaged. One or two of the onlookers were struck by the propeller before it came to rest but fortunately they were not seriously injured.

One is constantly amazed at the short take-off and landing performance of these old aircraft, which were able to operate from very small fields. Most of the reports say that they were airborne in a matter of 30 yards, which seems very hard to believe.

Hawker was interested in securing contracts for the supply of military aircraft to the Australian Government and made the most of any opportunities that arose. As a patriotic Australian, he would have felt a responsibility to see that the military chiefs and people in Government were made fully aware of the capabilities and need for aeroplanes in time of war. He had strong views about defence and spoke with some authority from his experience testing Sopwith aeroplanes for the Admiralty, and his attempt on the Round Britain flight.

His view was that the aeroplanes already imported for the Australian Defence Forces were unsuitable for their intended purpose. He was very much in favour of seaplanes, as any threat to Australia's shores would come from the sea. The aeroplanes which had been imported were, due to delays in delivery and assembly, already obsolete and now really only suited for pilot training. He pointed out that aviation was progressing so rapidly that the builders in England were producing two models a year, each model being a considerable improvement on its predecessor.

(Upper left) The Tabloid taking off down the straight at Caulfield Racecourse. The huge crowds were hard to control.

(Lower left) Hawker's Sopwith Tabloid took off after a run of about thirty yards. His passenger on this occasion was Miss Dixon.

(Upper) The Tabloid coming in to land at Elsternwick Golf Course.

The following Wednesday some more demonstration flying was arranged with the Minister of Defence, Senator Millen. Although this was kept secret as far as possible, a crowd gathered at New Street. Troubles were again experienced with the crowds. Hawker's father mounted a box to announce that there would be no flying until the people cleared the roadway. When this was eventually done Hawker was able to take off on a demonstration flight to show off the capabilities of the aeroplane.

Senator Millen, who Hawker had arranged to take for a flight, had great difficulty in getting past the police until he told them who he was. It was the first time a federal cabinet minister had made a flight in Australia. He was greatly impressed, much to Hawker's satisfaction, and said after his flight:

"I cannot say that there is any feature that one could describe as thrilling. Nothing can make one feel that one is heroic or any sort of a dare devil, it seems so beautifully simple, so steady and so safe. My flight with Hawker was one of the most enjoyable experiences I have had. Hawker is master of his machine and manipulates it with the greatest of ease. I have done a great deal of fast motoring from time to time, but there is no comparison between that and soaring in the air."

Other flights were made that day with Lt Harrison of the Australian Army, with Mr T.G. White, holder of the motor speed record between Adelaide and Melbourne, and Mr Francis Syme.

Friday turned out a beautiful day, so some flying was planned. Two ladies and two men enjoyed lengthy flights during the morning. One lady passenger remarked that she could plainly see the bottom of the bay while they were flying over Port Phillip. Hawker said that he and Kauper, while they were on the Round Britain flight, were able to see wrecks below the water along the coast of Scotland. Finally flying had to be called off for the day because there was no wind at all. The space available for landing was so short that at least a slight breeze was needed to operate safely. There was the usual trouble with the crowd. It was always a source of amazement how the public found out when flying was going to take place.

Hawker arranged to leave for Sydney on 17 February to demonstrate the art of aviation, and the Tabloid, to the other major centres in Australia. He felt that the more people who could be brought into contact with flying the better. He also wanted to set some flying records while he was in Australia, not only to bring flying more forcibly before the people but to bring Australia to the notice of the people in England.

The first demonstration in Sydney was made on Saturday, 28 February at Randwick racecourse, where 20,000 people had gathered. The Governor General, Lord Denman, was the first passenger and was taken up to 4,000 feet. The next was Miss

Shaking the Governor General's hand after taking him for a flight at Randwick Racecourse, Sydney. Note the dashboard instruments.

The official programme for the Sydney flights. It was overprinted for flights from the Albury Racecourse on 7 March 1914.

Strickland, the daughter of the Governor of New South Wales. After giving some less sedate demonstrations with Miss Dixon, whom he had taken up in Melbourne, he flew over to Victoria Park where he carried out some more passenger flying before returning to Randwick. There was some thought that he might attempt to loop the loop but this idea was abandoned because of the low cloud. On Sunday the show carried on with demonstration and passenger flights.

The Australian Height Record was the next challenge for Hawker. He had called at Albury to do some demonstration flying, which he did with his usual dash, from the Albury racecourse, after which he decided to make an altitude attempt. He reached a height of 7,800 feet, which broke the record but had a rather unfortunate ending.

Gliding down for a landing his engine stopped about 300 feet from the ground. When he was unable to restart it he was forced to land in a ploughed paddock near the racecourse but, due to the rough surface, the aeroplane stood on its nose and a dense cloud of dust rose into the air. Hawker, luckily, stepped out unhurt. Fortunately the machine was not badly damaged except for a broken propeller. His explanation for the engine stopping was that he had let it get cold on the descent and that it was pure carelessness on his part.

The damaged aeroplane was dismantled and sent back to Melbourne by road. Having arrived back in Melbourne on 11 March, the Tabloid was soon repaired and the propeller replaced with one of the spares he had brought out with him. It was ready for more flying and about 30 people had made arrangements to fly at a price of 20 pounds each. Flying continued from Elsternwick until early in April when Hawker took the aeroplane to Ballarat. Again large crowds gathered to watch his demonstrations.

Hawker had planned to give flying demonstrations in the gold fields area northwest of Melbourne, as a finale to his Australian tour. He had made about 60 flights so far and time must have been running out for the Gnome engine as there is no record of it having been overhauled, which was necessary about every 15 hours.

He made one demonstration flight before taking up one of the local residents. Unfortunately, when he was coming in to land, he could not avoid a hurdle that someone had left in the path he had selected to land on and the Tabloid was damaged. This ended his flying in Australia. The aeroplane was then dismantled and sent back to Melbourne by rail and road to the garage at Elsternwick, where it was boxed up for return to England. Final arrangements were made for passages for Hawker and Kauper back to England and the rest of their stay in Melbourne was taken up with visiting their families and friends.

After enjoying a very successful trip they embarked on the RMS *Mooltan* and arrived back in England on 6 June 1914.

(Right) The Sopwith Tabloid being repaired at Elsternwick after its crash on the racecourse at Albury. Note the side by side seating.

(Left) In a cloud of dust at the moment it nosed over, the Tabloid after landing at Albury Racecourse. Hawker stepped out unhurt.

Once more we have the benefit of Bob Chamberlain's records:

"There had been some advance publicity when Hawker and Kauper had discussions with newspaper reporters in Fremantle and Adelaide where the RMS *Maloja* had called. A civic reception had been arranged by residents at the St Kilda Town Hall in Melbourne.

"Harry had elected to stay with his parents at their home in Gourlay Street, Balaclava.

"George Hawker had much earlier closed down his works on the Nepean Highway at Wyckham Road and established a much smaller operation behind the house at Gourlay Street. I do not know the reason for this but he had brought some of the machinery, including two lathes and his steam plant, with him. The small workshop building had been divided into two sections. One part housed the engine and machinery and the other part the forge. The forge was operated by a very large hand-powered bellows.

"The purpose of the visit, obviously, was to try and sell Sopwith aircraft to the Australian Government, but Harry also took the opportunity to attend the wedding of his younger sister, Ruby.

"With them on the *Maloja*, Hawker and Kauper brought to Australia the finest performing plane in the world. This was the Tabloid. Harry Hawker had taken an important part in its design. Sopwiths at that time was a small company only employing about six men and had built only a few aircraft. Only the most elementary calculations had been made and the aircraft were drawn in chalk on the floor of the disused roller-skating rink rented by Tom Sopwith at Kingston on Thames.

"Harry's test flying of every plane he could get his hands on had convinced him that they could get good results from a more compact design than anything they had previously seen. Harry's skill at designing, with a good eye for best proportions and simplest constructions, seldom let him down.

"The little Tabloid biplane, with two side by side seats, had a wingspan of only 26 feet and a length of 25 feet. Even the earliest Sopwith aeroplanes were given type numbers, but because this biplane was small and compact the men working on its construction started referring to it as the Tabloid, and the name stuck. It was powered by an 80 hp French built, Gnome, rotary engine and had a speed range of 36 mph to 93 mph. The controls included a rudder bar and a control column, with a wheel to operate the wing-warp and elevators. Later versions had ailerons instead of the wing-warping system, which was obsolete even in 1914.

"The machine brought to Australia by Hawker and Kauper was the first of the type built and its performance was regarded as outstanding.

"Harry had brought with him from England all the trophies he had won and these included a magnificent silver model of the Round

Britain Sopwith seaplane. It was a large model, with a wing span of about 24 inches, and was in a glass case. I was really impressed, as was everybody else, with the great number of trophies all spread out on tables in the front parlour of the house.

"I recall the excitement of all concerned. The normally quiet, middle class, inner suburban street suddenly had cars and people everywhere and aeroplane talk was in the air. There were quite a lot of spare parts, including rigging wire and lots of turnbuckles with the Tabloid in the ship. There were structural parts, such as brackets made from high tensile sheet steel, cut out for low weight and bent to form. There were spare wheels and tyres as well as two spare propellers, at that period called tractors.

"Much of this material was left behind and was around for many years but all has now been lost, except for a new spare compass which I still have. The two spare propellers were not sufficient and a third was required later. It was made in Melbourne and after testing was stated by Harry to be satisfactory.

"Harry also brought with him the actual maps used for the Round Britain flight, I still have them today. They are pasted onto hard cardboard for handing back and forth between Hawker and Kauper, as they couldn't speak above the engine and wind noise. They wrote pencil notes on the maps and today they make amusing reading such as: 'Which way is north?', 'The engine is kicking', 'The exhaust pipe nut is loose.'

"Harry, with his restless spirit, wanted to start flying in Australia as soon as possible, but some delay was caused by customs while they tried to decide on the appropriate duty to apply to the castor oil needed to lubricate the rotary engine. Eventually the oil arrived at the Hawker home. It was in wooden barrels and we were surprised at the large quantity. It came on a horse drawn flat top lorry and was unloaded in the yard, to be picked up later by the garage service truck and taken to Elsternwick. I was interested to learn that the Gnome engine, with its radial rotating cylinders, was lubricated by a total loss system. The oil was regular medicinal castor oil and it was metered into the centre of the crankshaft by a small pump. The oil was then spread through the rotating engine by centrifugal force and out through the exhaust valves. A circular cowling at the front of the aircraft protected the upper part of the fuselage and an opening at the bottom of the cowling allowed the spray of oil, mixed with exhaust gas, to flow out where it made a sticky mess over the lower part of the aircraft. Even with the engine cowling it was inevitable that some of the castor oil mist could not be kept away from the pilot and passenger causing some inconvenience.

"As soon as the lubricating oil arrived Harry was ready to make the first flight. The aircraft had been assembled less its wings, inside the garage, but it was necessary for the wings to be fitted after the

Bob Chamberlain's vivid memories are supported by this picture of the Tabloid outside the garage at Elsternwick Junction in January 1914.

aircraft had been brought out through the doors and was on the apron outside the building.

"Hawker and Kauper were experts at rigging the aircraft, they had to remove the wings and reinstall them every time the machine went through the garage doorway, and they did it very quickly.

"It was 28 January 1914 and the lubricating oil had arrived the day before. The Tabloid was wheeled out onto New Street. The engine was primed (they called it doped) through the open exhaust valves with petrol from a syringe. The fixed crankshaft was positioned with the crankpin in a vertical position, which caused the exhaust valves to open when the cylinders were near the bottom opening in the cowl.

"About six men held on to the interplane struts and the tail assembly while the engine was run up. When the men were signalled to let go the Tabloid ran a short distance before becoming airborne. It cleared the street wiring which was on both sides of the road, some electric wires actually crossing the road.

"After climbing to 5,000 feet, being out of sight and amongst the clouds some of the time, the Tabloid was put through some steeply banked turns and spiralled down to land on the golf links.

"To get the aircraft out it was necessary for part of the fence to be dismantled. It was covered with wire mesh to prevent golf balls hitting traffic on the roadway. The owners would not agree to dismantling the fence to let the aircraft in but after the masterful take-off from the street and the flying demonstration, their attitude changed. From that time onwards the golf links was the aerodrome. At best this was a hazardous situation with trees and sand traps. The landings were not always free from damage to the undercarriage.

"When Harry decided to take off from New Street, Maurice Shmith and some old workmates from Tarrant Motors Company arrived to watch the flight. The men from Tarrants also acted as traffic controllers and stopped everything while the aircraft took off.

"The *Australian Motorist* dated 2 February 1914, carried a headline 'Harry Hawker Ascends from the Street', stating, 'The outstanding feature of Mr Hawker's flight on 27 January was the ascent from the street opposite the garage. Hitherto a wide open field was considered necessary for aviation and whilst this may be so to effect a safe landing, it is conclusively proved that in the hands of a capable aviator a modern aircraft can ascend from outside our front door. Hawker reached an altitude of 5,000 feet, but at times he came down sufficiently to permit his engine being heard. He covered the southern suburbs and descended by a volplane into the golf links. He touched earth and landed like a bird.'

"The *Australian Motorist* commenting on 'Aviation in Australia' in their issue of 2 March 1914 stated, 'The young aviator, he is only 22 years of age, scored a great triumph. His predecessors, Houdini, Hammond, MacDonald and Hart, had given aerial demonstrations that had been recorded successful but none of them had attempted the daring feats that Hawker accomplished. His manoeuvres were of a totally different standard. It was as the difference between an amateur and a professional. Hawker impressed everyone with the fact that he possessed complete mastery over his machine.'

"A few earlier fliers had managed to get off the ground in Australia but their performance had not created much interest and were regarded as hops, rather than flights.

"During Harry's visit to Australia he did not take any member of his family for a flight. My mother told me later that Harry's brother, Bert, was disappointed at not having a flight. The only private, non paying, passenger was Harry's old friend and motorcycle racing associate, Cecil De Fraga.

"Lt Eric Harrison, an old friend of Hawker's, went to England in 1911 to qualify for his pilot's certificate under the rules of the Royal Aero Club. On 12 September 1911 he received his certificate, number 131. Hawker qualified a year later on 17 September 1912, certificate number 297. Harrison returned to Australia ready to fly but could not get any action from the Defence Department to provide aircraft.

"Bristol Boxkites and Deperdussin monoplanes had been ordered two years earlier and had arrived in Melbourne one year after being ordered, but were still not unpacked. The Defence Department could not be stirred into action until Lt Harrison had taken his first trip aloft as a passenger in Harry's plane. The publicity of this flight stirred the department into action. Temporary canvas hangars were erected near the Geelong Road, at Laverton.

"The Boxkites and Deperdussins were taken out and assembled. These planes were obsolete but Harrison was soon flying the Boxkites and one of his first pupils to pass his pilot's tests in Australia was Richard Williams who, later, as Air Marshall 'Dicky' Williams, became the highly respected head of the Royal Australian Air Force. Williams, many years later, told me that they were never able to fly the Deperdussins but could use them for practice at engine starting as their three cylinder Anzani radial engines would oil up their spark plugs before they could get airborne. (One of these machines is now in the War Memorial Museum at Canberra.)

"In spite of his great workload, Harry took a few days off to go to Caramut for a day's shooting with his old boss Ernest De Little. Harry, following in his father's footsteps as a first rate rifle shot, enjoyed his trip to Caramut with the company of De Little and other friends. Although he was offered the use of up-to-date cars, Harry elected to drive there in his father's old, worn out Cotton-Desgouttes.

"When Harry arrived back in Australia to promote interest in the Tabloid he appointed, as manager, a man named Sculthorpe to organize his program, interstate travel, and suitable sites for flying. It was Sculthorpe who arranged for him to fly from the Caulfield

(Melbourne) racecourse on 5 February 1914.

"I travelled with the garage crew on the old chain drive flat top Lacre lorry which was the regular garage recovery and service vehicle. Spare wheels for the aircraft, petrol and a barrel of castor oil for the engine, were included in the equipment.

"A section of the straight had been selected for take-off and landing. There was not much space to spare, even though the Tabloid would be airborne after only a short run. It was, as usual, held back by about six men while the engine was run up. On landing, strategically placed men would run out and hold on to the interplane struts as no brakes were fitted. After a few flights it became apparent that the crowd could not be controlled. They just could not understand that clear space was required for landing the aeroplane.

"After some hazardous landings several men were slightly injured and, during his last landing on the racecourse, the undercarriage and propeller were damaged but not to an extent that the plane couldn't fly.

"It was obvious that no further landings could be made at Caulfield. Miss Ruby Dixon, who was awaiting her turn as passenger, climbed into the Tabloid with Harry who took-off and, after a few manoeuvres in an endeavour to give the crowd some compensation for their travel and entry fee, headed for the golf links at Elsternwick where he made a difficult landing adding to the damage already done to the aircraft.

"As was the regular procedure the wings were removed and the Tabloid taken into the garage. The propeller was damaged and a spare installed. Repairs were made to the undercarriage and a test flight made with take-off and landing at the golf links.

"I was present only at the flights in Melbourne but listened in to the constant talk at home. Harry's flights in Australia, and his discussions with the many visitors, were always of great interest to me and I would go over most of it with my parents who, of course, were living at their own home nearby but were fairly constant visitors at the Hawkers. The aircraft was kept at my father's C.L.C. Garage and Engineering Works, where not much motor work was done while it was there. Harry, like all members of the Hawker family, was always busy. He took very little notice of me as a 6 year old and we had few talks, but he didn't seem to mind when I would listen in to his conversations.

"Just a few years earlier, Adolphe Pegoud had astounded the pilots in England with his masterful exhibition of stunt flying at Brooklands. He had, with a specially modified Bleriot monoplane, done loops, tailslides, rolls and inverted flying. It is said that Pegoud flew across the airstrip at Brooklands inverted at a height of only about 30 feet. Visitors often seemed to want to discuss looping the loop with Harry and would attempt to get him to make a commitment to do it with the Sopwith Tabloid. He avoided this and did not loop the aircraft in Australia. He obviously had a reason for this but didn't ever explain, he just avoided giving any assurances about it. However, on his return to England, he made some modifications to the Tabloid, which was the first one built. Harry then took it up to about 10,000 feet and made 12 successive loops.

"On 21 February 1914 Harry had the repaired Tabloid in Sydney. He sent it from Melbourne by train, seeing no point in flying 500 miles over areas where few people would see it. His Melbourne tour manager, Sculthorpe, had been replaced by Claud Kingston who had wide experience managing theatre promotions.

"Kingston had, after some difficulty, persuaded the management of Randwick racecourse to hire the property for a series of Hawker flights. At Caulfield the big unruly crowd had damaged some equipment and the Randwick management feared that they could face the same problems. However, Kingston persuaded them otherwise and a fair price was agreed for use of the racecourse.

"A surprise of the day was when the Governor General, Lord Denman had a flight. He apparently discussed this in Melbourne when Harry landed at Government House.

"Hawker, also while in Sydney, flew from the Victoria Park racecourse, taking up paying passengers from each location. The flights from Victoria Park were delayed by rain but otherwise the program went through without problems.

"Many years later my father told me the real reason for the crash at Albury was that the engine had lost all its power. In the excitement of the day they had forgotten to top up the tank and the engine simply ran out of fuel. A fuel gauge of a crude type was on the aircraft, but it would seem that Harry didn't depend on it thinking that he had started with a full tank. The machine was brought back to Melbourne by train and repaired at the C.L.C. Garage.

"Repairs to the Tabloid involved fitting a new propeller. The original and both spares had been damaged. Arrangements were made with James Moore and Sons in Melbourne to make a new propeller, laminated from French walnut and hand forming the contours to the correct shape using templates made from one of the originals. Engine mountings were distorted and quite a lot of work was done before the Tabloid could take the air again.

"Much interest and a lot of publicity resulted from the Harry Hawker visit to Australia with the first sophisticated aircraft to reach this country. However, no orders resulted from the great effort. Hawker had done everything possible to convince the Defence Department that they required something better than the obsolete machines they had. Nobody in authority could appreciate the value of aircraft defence. Harry's old friend, Maurice Shmith, by then a man of some influence, tried unsuccessfully to get an order for the

A serene and picturesque photograph of Hawker flying the Sopwith Tabloid over Albert Park Lake, Melbourne, in the late afternoon.

Tabloid. The success of the second Tabloid in winning the Schneider Trophy seemed only to strengthen the authorities' view that such machines were too sophisticated for Australia and they ordered Maurice Farman Pusher training planes. It was in one of these machines that I first flew in 1919 (at age 11) after it had been sold to Graham Carey.

"My recollection of the Harry Hawker visit is mainly of the enormous amount of work by all concerned. In addition to all the work on the aircraft, which included removing the wings each time the machine had to go into the garage, installing and re-rigging them each time flights were made from Elsternwick, a lot of work was necessary as a result of accidental damage. The crash at Albury necessitated a good deal of straightening out and making of new parts. However, it was agreed that the Australian visit had been thoroughly successful and had created interest in flying as a serious development.

"The Tabloid was packed and in early May 1914 returned with Hawker and Kauper to England on the RMS *Mooltan*. Harry kept up a reasonable flow of correspondence with my mother and father after he returned to England and as he had done from the time he went to Sopwiths, sent copies of *Flight* and the *Aeroplane*, as well as photos and newspaper cuttings.

"Harry's flying career sometimes came into conversations, even many years after his death. My father had been one of the small group of young engineering men of action and they spoke the same language. He talked a great deal with Harry about the motoring and aviation scene in England and Australia."

Chapter Six

War Clouds

Harry Hawker arrived back in England on Saturday, 6 June 1914 and the very next day was flying at Brooklands. As he had not flown since the crash at Bendigo, Australia, at the end of March, he could not get back into the air quickly enough.

He added one more feature to his repertoire after his return to England when, ten days after his return, he looped the loop several times. When the Tabloid was being repaired he had the fabric covering removed from the rear section of the fuselage, as he felt that this would make it more manageable while executing this manoeuvre. His performances always thrilled the crowds who attended the many air meetings that had become a very popular spectator sport at that time. Large crowds gathered at both Brooklands and Hendon.

There were quite a number of flying accidents but, fortunately, pilots often walked away from them unhurt, or with comparatively minor injuries, and were soon flying again. The aircraft, often seemingly badly damaged, were repaired in a matter of days and were soon fit to take to the air again. It was possibly thanks to the flimsy construction that there were not more serious injuries. The energy of the crash was probably absorbed sufficiently slowly with the crumpling of the aircraft structure.

The following account of another of Hawker's accidents is typical of the day and was printed in the *Aeroplane* of 1 July 1914.

"One of the most extraordinary accidents in aviation, and a still more remarkable escape from death, occurred to Mr Harry Hawker at Brooklands on Saturday evening last. Mr Hawker went up about 7 pm in the Sopwith Scout (100 hp Gnome) and, at about 1,200 feet, he made one of his famous loops with the engine cut off, by diving steeply and then pulling back. He made the loop perfectly, but over the Byfleet Road, as he came out of it, he started a vertical dive with a spin in it.

"When I first caught sight of him from the paddock he was doing a perfect tourbillon spin, that is to say the wings were revolving round the centre line of the fuselage, and the machine was standing vertically on its nose. It was coming down quite slowly for such a fast machine, the pace being nothing like its ordinary diving speed. Then the tail seemed to swing out and the vertical path became an irregular spiral to the right, until finally the machine seemed to be doing a banked turn with the fuselage nearly horizontal and the left wing up. The speed of descent had by then decreased noticeably, but it was obvious that the machine was not under proper control, for it seemed to flutter round like a falling leaf. At this point it disappeared behind the trees on St George's Hill.

"As quickly as possible a number of people from Brooklands rushed to the spot and, after considerable difficulty, found the machine on the ground in a thick coppice, with Mr Hawker standing alongside it absolutely unhurt. A few minutes afterwards he went off back to Brooklands, sitting on the carrier of a motor cycle, leaving the machine in charge of the Sopwith machine crew.

"Apparently the machine had struck partly sideways and partly nose-on into the top of a tall tree, into which it had flown rather than fallen. It had then fallen vertically, bringing several big boughs of the tree with it, and had finally sat down right side up, flat on its chassis, on top of sundry saplings and undergrowth. The wings had folded up neatly as it fell through the trees, and had come down like a lid on the cockpit. How Mr Hawker got out is a mystery. The chassis had telescoped into the front of the fuselage. The cowl was dented and bent, but not torn off. Two or three valve tappets had been wiped off the engine, which was evidently revolving when it struck the trees. The propeller was broken at the ends, but not at the boss. The fuselage, aft of the tank, together with the elevator and rudder, were absolutely untouched.

"The first thing we did was to test the controls, and found the elevator and rudder working perfectly. The warp wires were also undamaged, so there can be no question of controls going wrong. What then, was the cause of the accident?

"For some time previously, Mr Hawker had been proving the extraordinary stability of this machine. He used to take it up to a thousand feet or so, switch off the engine, and let the machine glide. Then he would apply back stick slowly to stall it. With the controls hard back it would neither tailslide, nor dive, or sideslip. It would simply descend on an even keel like a parachute, but moving gently forward and rolling slowly first to one side and then back to the other. Occasionally, in a gust, it would slide to one side, descending sideways at about 45 degrees, in a side slip. On moving the stick forward it would pick up its gliding angle promptly. In fact it seemed absolutely stable in every direction. It recovered promptly also from a straight dive which was almost vertical.

"Now comes the smash, and it is worth studying. The nose did not appear to come up as expected when the stick was moved back. During the afternoon Mr Hawker had been arguing with an officer of

Hawker at Hendon. Note the extra forward wheel to prevent the aircraft tipping forward.

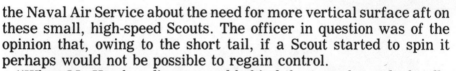

(Right) The Sopwith Tabloid aeroplane, the first of the fighting scouts, designed by Hawker. It was modified for looping the loop after his return from Australia.

the Naval Air Service about the need for more vertical surface aft on these small, high-speed Scouts. The officer in question was of the opinion that, owing to the short tail, if a Scout started to spin it perhaps would not be possible to regain control.

"When Mr Hawker disappeared behind the trees he undoubtedly had his stick right back and, as he was then banked well over to the right, his elevators were acting as if they were rudders, and so were forcing his tail round and increasing the spin. In this position the rudder should act as an elevator and throw the nose of the machine down, so causing a straight nose dive from which it should be easy to recover. Mr Hawker tells me he tried to do this, but could not get it round against the air pressure. He puts this down to the rudder being of the unbalanced type. He thinks that with a balanced rudder and no fin he could have done it.

"Also, he admits that if he had moved the stick forward after application of rudder, as soon as he found the spin developing, and had made a straight dive, he could have pulled up straight, but he thought he was too near the ground to risk doing so.

"It must be remembered that the Caudron aeroplane, in which Chanteloup does his tourbillon dive, has a tail that warps in unison with the wings and that it has two, big balanced rudders, so that it really has more control than the Scout class and, as it is a much slower machine, it changes its attitude in a much shorter distance

110

even if it takes the same length of time to do so. Still, it looked to me as if Mr Hawker was getting the machine under control just as she disappeared, and I believe that if he tries the experiment again at 3,000 feet, instead of 1,000, he will have regained control before reaching 1,000 feet.

"Anyhow he is very lucky to be alive, and only for that opportune clump of trees he would not have been. Still, to please the Navy, it might be worthwhile trying one of the Scouts with a bigger rudder and fin, and a proportionately strong rudder tube, so as to see how it affects their normal flying. If it does not slow the machine appreciably, it might be well to adopt the larger size simply to give extra directional stability and control, and simplify the flying of the type by less clever chaps.

"Has it struck anybody that there may be a very good reason for the old Antoinette system of having vertical fins and rudders exactly equal to the tail fins and elevators?"

Some of these accidents were the result of flying conditions that were, at that time, not fully understood, or due to shortcomings in the design of the aeroplane. This was only to be expected with the state of knowledge at that time. It was only because of people like Hawker that these problems became recognised and understood. The engines of the day were not very powerful and sometimes incapable of providing enough thrust for the aeroplane to climb out of an unfavourable situation.

The foregoing account of Hawker's accident is typical of others where loss of control occurred. This one appeared to develop into what is now termed a "flat spin". When this occurs the fixed fin and the vertical control surfaces can be shielded from the relative upward and sideways airflow by the elevator, thus reducing their effectiveness to the extent that the rotation about the vertical axis of the aeroplane cannot be arrested.

A record of the incident by fellow Australian, Horrie Miller, who arrived with the search party, relates that Hawker was obviously lost in contemplation shortly afterwards.

"...Again he was in the cockpit, reliving the moments of suspense and panic, the struggle to defeat the unknown, the last despairing burst of engine power and the plunge to earth. 'I know what I should have done.' He paused. We hung on his words. 'If only I'd had the guts to do it...I'll have a new plane ready in 4 days. I'll get into a spin and get out of it.' All eyes followed him as he turned away.

"I helped put the finishing touches to that new plane. It was similar, except for the engine, to the one in which Hawker had crashed and, like all Sopwith's landplanes of that time, it had been brought by truck for assembly at Brooklands.

"I was there to swing the propeller on that mist-laden morning of the fateful test. As St George, in ages past, had slain the Dragon, so Hawker, a modern knight, leather jacket and goggles in place of shining armour, would renew the encounter in which he had been vanquished a few days earlier. Again, over St George's Hill, the battle was to be joined and no quarter given. The miracle of escape could not be repeated.

"There were no spectators beside myself. Hawker, cap on back to front, goggles ready, stood quietly beside the plane as I turned the propeller. He took a long look around and up into the sky, then swung his body into the cockpit. 'I'll go to 8,000 feet, get into a spin and come out.' 'Switch-off! — Suck in! — Contact!' With the cloud of white smoke usual to a rotary engine, she started at once. Hawker ran the engine up to full revs then waved for 'chocks away'. The roar of the engine brought a few sleepy people out of their beds. The plane swung into a graceful bank at the end of the airfield up into the cold morning air. Hawker was part of this sweet, new plane, with its smell of fresh varnish. How beautifully she climbed above the ground haze! There lay the misty Thames, 4,000 feet beneath. A lifetime yet to swing up into the lovely morning sky. There was the oval saucer of Brooklands and the forest. How comforting the motor's steady beat! Only that dull ache of anxiety, this thing that must be done against every natural instinct. Six thousand feet. Away to the left lay the mighty city, London, in its blanket of smoke and, further on the sea, the land a mosaic of villages, roads, railways and pastures. He cut the petrol a little as the mixture became richer.

"Seven thousand feet, one thousand to go. It was growing cold but at this great height he met the enemy on better terms, eight thousand. Over with the stick, on with the rudder. Cut the motor! She whipped into the spin, nose down, wings whirling down and down. The earth was a spinning bowl beneath. What to do now? Is this the moment? Push the stick forward, not back. Every nerve rebelled against this desperate action. The nose was down, must one send it further down? Perhaps, after all one does not have the guts. Down she goes. Forward with the stick down, centralize the rudder, hold.

"How sweet the glide, the long, sweet glide. He turned a little, gently dipped the wing. Where was the wind? Ah yes - the smoke from the chimneys. Softly the wheels touched the grass, the battle fought and won.

"Hawker had mastered the spinning dive."

It is interesting to observe that all through the references to aeroplanes in the early days control surfaces were frequently found to be inadequate and modifications often had to be made. Even on the Sopwith Snipe, enlarged ailerons had to be fitted. In the light of later knowledge the rudder and fin areas of the aeroplanes of that era were completely inadequate. This was particularly the case on aeroplanes having rotary engines, where the gyroscopic forces needed to be controlled in addition to the aerodynamic.

From the descriptions of some of the accidents where the aeroplane came into contact with trees on the approach for landing it seems unlikely that they were aware of the significance of wind shear. Some explanation of this may be of interest. It is quite usual when a stiff wind is blowing that a layer of air, above the retarding effect of trees and other low obstructions, can have a velocity of 15 mph, or more, greater than the velocity on the actual landing field. The wind shear is the separation between these two layers moving at different speeds, and the transition can be quite sharp.

An aeroplane approaching for a landing into the wind is, for example, travelling at a speed through the air 10 mph above its stalling speed. Should the wind shear be 15 mph, the relative speed of the aeroplane through the air becomes, very suddenly, less than its stalling speed and it simply stops flying and stalls into the ground. Experience teaches one to recognize the times when wind shear may be present and when to take appropriate action but, as air is not visible, the existence and extent of this phenomenon is not easily assessed. It is one of the problems dealt with very fully in modern flight training programs.

The early aeroplanes were, in many cases, not particularly stable in flight. As time went by, improvements were made to take some of the strain off the pilot. When Hawker returned from his Australian trip he obviously thought there was room for improvement in lateral

One of the best head and shoulders pictures of Harry Hawker, signed by him in 1916.

stability on the Tabloid so he changed the rigging by introducing a dihedral angle on the lower wings. This is the upward angle given to each wing. It confers an inherent lateral stability which tends to restore the wings to a level attitude after any disturbance.

Hawker continued with his flying activities and gave demonstrations of looping the loop at air shows, which were now being held at Hendon because of the increasing use of Brooklands for testing war planes. He is reputed to have been the first person to loop a seaplane.

The use of rotary engines, in which the crankshaft is fixed into the airframe structure, was widespread, especially later during World War I. These engines rotated around the fixed crankshaft, the propeller being attached to the front of the crankcase. Although they were extremely light, the mass of crankcase and cylinders, rotating at 1,100 to 1,200 rpm, was enough to introduce control problems of their own.

There were conflicting opinions about the most suitable type of engine for fitting to aircraft. Both types of engine, the in-line and the rotary, were at about the same stage of development, although there was probably a greater acceptance of the in-line, water-cooled engine, because it had been in use in motorcars for some time. It had a greater life between overhauls and was probably more reliable at that stage but its weight per unit of power was greater, and weight of course was very important. It was also more vulnerable to gunfire. French and German opinion leaned towards the in-line while the air-cooled rotary was generally more favoured by the British.

Sopwith's design philosophy for the fighter type was one where maximum agility was required. They therefore chose the air-cooled rotary engine, of which several were available such as the Gnome, Le Rhone and Clerget with a range of horsepowers up to 130.

Rotary engines had two great advantages for aircraft, apart from their light weight. They were short, fore and aft, and could be placed much closer to the centre of gravity of the aeroplane resulting in a much shorter, close-coupled aeroplane which was much quicker in manoeuvring. They were also lighter because they did not carry the additional weight of water jackets, radiators and cooling water. They had a further weight advantage because the engine which rotated round the crankshaft was fixed solidly to the firewall and bulkhead at the front of the aeroplane.

The early rotary engines, Gnome, Le Rhone and Clerget did have serious cooling problems because the cylinders were machined from steel billets. As the engine rotated the front and forward side of the cylinder ran cooler than the rest which caused it to warp out of the true circle. This caused problems with piston sealing which could only be overcome by providing "L" shaped bronze piston rings at the top of the piston, called "obturator" rings. Bronze was the only metal that could adapt to the warped shape but was unable to cope with the temperatures to which it was subjected for long periods. They did not have a long life and engines usually had to be pulled down and re-ringed every 12 to 15 hours. If a ring failed during flight it often caused a fire and many pilots and aircraft were lost as result of this.

All aeroplanes fitted with rotary engines suffered a common problem known as "gyroscopic precession". This was as a result of the rotating mass of the engine. Any change in direction of the aircraft changed the rotational plane of the engine. This caused a force to act at right angles to that change in direction. This had to be compensated for by the pilot and was the cause of many losses during the early stages of training.

Another problem was caused by lifting the tail in the early part of the take-off run resulted in a strong tendency for the aeroplane to veer to the left. This was called gyroscopic kick by the pilots and unless positive and early corrective action was taken with the rudder, a disaster would follow. Full right rudder was used at the beginning of the take-off until the tail was up. When flying speed was reached, and the nose raised to climb away, this force acted in the opposite direction which resulted in many spectacular and sometimes disastrous turns to the right immediately after take-off. This was particularly dangerous as, at this stage, the air speed had not built up to the point where anything but the gentlest turn could be undertaken without an aerodynamic stall resulting.

These aeroplanes were, therefore, somewhat tricky to fly until one mastered their idiosyncrasies. Once in the air the effects of the gyroscopic forces were ever present. The aircraft could turn very quickly to the right and very slowly to the left. So much so that, if one wished to turn 90 degrees left, it was almost quicker to do a 270 degree turn right to end up on the same heading.

Chapter Seven

Design and Testing

In the summer of 1914 the clouds of war were gathering with increasing speed. The factories were now working with feverish activity to design, and then produce, aeroplanes for this emergency. When war was declared on 4 August 1914 Sopwiths were in a leading position to expand into mass production. However they were not able to supply the numbers required and some production of Sopwith aeroplanes was organized in other factories, many of which had no previous experience in aircraft construction. The infant aircraft industry was faced with an expansion of unprecedented magnitude.

Sopwiths had designed several aeroplanes to offer the Services. The one that was built initially in the greatest numbers was the One and a Half Strutter, which will be referred to from now on simply as the Strutter. It was built in single and two-seater versions. Over 5,466 of these were produced. Sopwiths built 246, 1,020 were built by eight other British factories and a remaining 4,200 were built by the French.

The other aircraft delivered in numbers was the Sopwith Pup, a single-seater fighter. It was more agile than the Strutter having a shorter wing span of 26 feet 6 inches and more specifically designed for air combat. A total of 1,847 were built, 97 by Sopwiths and the rest by other British factories. It carried a single Vickers gun firing through the propeller arc and was fitted with the Sopwith-Kauper gun interruptor gear to prevent the bullets hitting the propeller blades. The Pup was the closest progenitor of the Camel.

The vast amount of organizing and liaison that was required between Sopwiths and the factories building their aircraft would have been Hawker's responsibility. He also managed to do a considerable amount of test flying and supervision of construction standards.

This would have been extremely difficult in the case of the factories in France, which had little previous experience in aeroplane production, and which worked with the metric system of measurement. All the Sopwith drawings were in imperial measurements and the conversion to metric, or the adoption of imperial by the French, must have caused problems.

In 1911 consideration was being given to the establishment of units dedicated to the use of the aeroplane in warfare. Agreement was reached and Royal approval of the title "Royal Flying Corps" was given in March 1912. The RFC formed two groups with a common central flying school: the RFC Naval Wing and RFC Military Wing. Shortly after, the Naval Wing became the Royal Naval Air Service and the RFC dropped the word "military".

Initially it was planned that the RNAS would play the major role in the fighting in France and the RFC would handle home defence. Due to the rapid development of the war it was not long before the units of the RFC moved to France where both services worked in close cooperation.

The association between Sopwiths and the RNAS probably arose initially because of Tom Sopwith's affinity for boats and his early interest in building seaplanes and flying boats.

The RNAS were also very interested in the possible use of aeroplanes based on ships and a great many trials were carried out which, because of their superior short take-off performance, were done with Sopwith machines. Hawker was deeply involved with these trials which began with the Schneiders and Strutters fitted with two floats. These could only be launched and recovered in reasonably calm weather conditions as they had to be lowered from ships into the sea and then recovered after their flight.

The Cunard liner *Campania* was used in the North Sea as a mother ship for this work, during which time Hawker became friendly with a navigator, Lt Cdr K. Mackenzie Grieve, of whom he formed such a high opinion that he invited him to accompany him as navigator, after the war, when he made the attempt to be first to cross the Atlantic Ocean by air nonstop.

It was decided to build a launching platform over the gun turrets on HMS *Furious* as it was essential to develop a system in which landplanes could be used without the ship having to heave to lower their aircraft as this manoeuvre provided a stationary target for any lurking German submarines. The platform idea was to steam full speed into the wind so the combined velocity of the wind and the forward speed of the ship would allow the aeroplane to take off and touch down at a relatively low deck speed.

It was not until August 1917 that the first successful shipboard landing was made by Sqn Cdr Dunning on HMS *Furious*. This was a very hazardous procedure as he had to fly round the funnel before lining up with the platform to touch down. It did at least prove that the idea was feasible. The second attempt was less successful and Dunning unfortunately drowned. The platform was then extended over the gun barrels before further trials were made.

The battleship HMS *Repulse* and the light cruiser HMS *Yarmouth* were also fitted with platforms and Flt Cdr Rutland, using a Sopwith

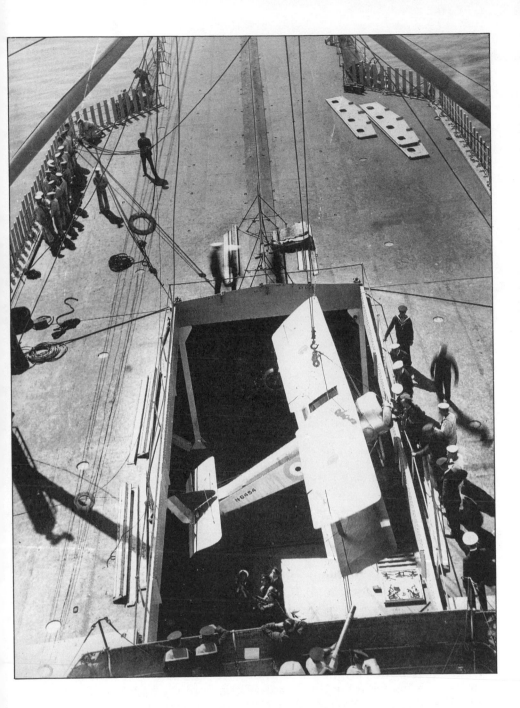

Hoisting a Strutter from the hold during sea trials — a tight fit.

Strutter, made the first successful trials. Later on, in April 1918, HMAS *Australia* was fitted with a turret platform and launched its first aeroplane.

Towards the end of the war these trials led to the construction of the first flush deck aircraft carrier, HMS *Argus*, on which the funnels and upper works were displaced to one side to allow the aeroplanes a direct approach for landings and to provide a longer deck length both for take-off and landing. She was converted from an Italian passenger liner, the *Conto Rosso*, and carried 18 Sopwith Cuckoos, which were equipped to carry torpedoes. However, the war ended before she could be used.

The relatively small number of aeroplanes produced by Sopwiths at Kingston on Thames indicated that they were concentrating on the design of advanced fighters. Tom Sopwith has said that Hawker was largely responsible for the design of the Camel which was the most successful fighter of World War I. It was the first Sopwith aeroplane to be design stressed and all previous aeroplanes had been built by rule of thumb. As time went by, the increasing demands on the airframe made it necessary to adopt a more professional engineering approach to design and stress. The results of this show

(Left) A Strutter taking off from a launch platform erected over the forward gun turret and gun barrels of HMS Furious.

up in the comparison between the Strutter and the Pup on the one hand, and the Camel on the other.

Basically the Camel was similar to the Strutter and the Pup, but was designed to carry increased firepower. It was fitted with two Vickers machine guns firing through the propeller arc. This resulted in increased weight as the second machine gun weighed 88 lbs, plus its ammunition supply.

The Camel had a reputation for being very tricky to fly but it was a very agile aeroplane which, in part, was due to the concentration of weight over a very short space, fore and aft of the centre of gravity. This agility was the reason it was such a successful fighter as it could outmanoeuvre the enemy who were mostly flying aeroplanes with in-line, water-cooled engines.

The reason for this was that it was the first aeroplane to be design stressed which resulted in a more efficient use of materials and hence a better power to weight ratio.

Again, a large part of the production of the Camel was farmed out. Sopwiths built a total of 503 out of a total of 5,597. The main subcontractors were Boulton and Paul, who produced 1,550, and Ruston Proctor, 1,573.

Two boats coming to the rescue of a Sopwith Pup ditched at sea.

(Insert) A Sopwith Pup landing on the deck of HMS Furious, *an early aircraft carrier.*

The design changes that created the Camel were no doubt brought about by Hawker's close liaison with the squadrons who were flying Strutters and Pups in action over the Western Front. He made frequent trips over to France, to various operational centres and to the French factories, to test fly the aeroplanes they were producing.

A few Camels were converted to dual control by placing another cockpit behind the standard one so that pilots could get the feel of the aeroplane before going solo.

A comparison between the Strutter and the Camel shows the progress that had been made in design. The Camel was considerably smaller. It had a wing span of 28 feet against the Strutter's 33½ feet. This gave the Camel a much better rate of roll. As the Camel was lighter overall, in spite of carrying the extra machine gun and ammunition, it could climb at twice the rate of the Strutter and though not much faster on the level, could manoeuvre more rapidly.

The comparison in the following table has been made between the Mark of each type having a 130 hp Clerget engine.

	Empty weight lbs	All up weight lbs	Max speed mph	Rate of climb mins to 10,000 ft
Strutter	1,305	2,150	97	17.8
Pup	780/850	1,234/1,290	104	14.5/12.5
Camel	929	1,482	105	8.5

The Pup was the true progenitor of the Camel, as it was strictly a single-seater fighter equipped with either a Le Rhone or a Clerget 80 hp engine except for one Mark which had a 100 hp Gnome Monosoupape engine.

Weight saved in the design of aircraft, consistent with strength, has a snowballing effect because this, in turn, reduces the strain on components, which can then be made lighter.

A problem which appeared to affect the Sopwith aircraft more than others, particularly the Strutter and the Pup, was gun stoppages. This was due to the fact that the Sopwiths, with their superior performance, were capable of climbing to higher altitudes, thus encountering lower temperatures. Height was of great importance in aerial fighting for two reasons: it placed the anti-aircraft gunners at a greater disadvantage; and to be above the enemy planes when attacking was a great advantage.

Another Australian H.C. (Horrie) Miller, for whom Hawker had secured a job with Sopwiths just before the war, visited the factory at Kingston. He had joined up shortly after war broke out and was a pilot in the Australian Flying Corps. He said it was like entering a new world with the expansion that had taken place with thousands of workers, nearly half of them women, turning out row after row of new fighters. Hawker was able to find time in his busy schedule to take Miller down to Brooklands where he had worked before joining up. While they were together Miller impressed on Hawker the absolute necessity to attain height in aerial combat, that he could always out-climb the German aeroplane but could not match him in a dive.

(Horrie Miller was later to become famous as the founder of the MacRobertson Miller Airline in Western Australia, one of the pioneer airlines which established and maintained regular air services in Western Australia for many years.)

Machine guns in aircraft run into many problems caused by high flying where the temperatures were lower. One of the problems was that the viscosity of the lubricating oils increased which demanded more recoil of the gun bolt. In the rarefied atmosphere, the gas energy imparted to the recoiling portion of the guns was, in fact, reduced. This combination of effects sometimes failed to force the bolt back far enough to complete the reloading cycle, resulting in the stoppages. In addition, it only required a defective round, in which the charge burned slightly slower, to cause the bullet to strike a propeller blade. This was a problem inherent in all guns firing forward through the propellers.

(Hawker's old friend Harry Kauper was an inventor of one of the most reliable systems designed to allow guns to fire, by means of an interrupter gear, through the propeller blades without hitting them. Kauper later went on to achieve further recognition for his work in the development of radio communications in outback Australia.)

The solution to this problem gave the Camel its name. A pronounced hump, forward of the cockpit, was built as a cowling covering the breeches of the machine guns and extending forward to the engine. This conveyed hot air from the engine to the guns which kept the working parts warm. The hydraulic lines from the gun interruptor generator on the engine to the machine gun firing mechanism were also subject to the effects of the freezing temperatures, again resulting in sluggish gun operation.

In early designs the feed belts for the forward firing Vickers machine guns were made of canvas which absorbed moisture when the aircraft was on the ground. In the below freezing temperatures encountered as the aircraft climbed, they froze — another cause of stoppages. There was also the problem of stowing that part of the canvas belt from which the ammunition had been extracted. Later, the metallic clip machine gun belt was designed and put into production which overcame this problem. When the spent ammunition was discharged from the gun breech the belt linkage disintegrated and the links and the spent shells were simply jettisoned through chutes into the air.

The standard Vickers machine gun (designed for ground use) fed from the right-hand side and the empty shells discharged from the left side. Problems, of course, arose when it came to installing two guns in the narrow space available in the aircraft as it was difficult to arrange the feed chute on one side. One of the guns discharged shells near the centre line of the aircraft which required a special chute which had to be arranged so that it cleared the feed of the other gun.

The munitions factories were so heavily involved in producing machine guns for the army it was naturally very difficult to get them to produce guns with left-handed feed blocks. However these finally became available, which simplified the installation considerably.

The Lewis guns used by the observers in the rear cockpit of the Strutters, were fed from drum magazines. Initially they were limited to 47 rounds. However, it was not a very difficult job to add another deck and double their capacity.

Hawker, on his visits to the squadrons, was made well aware of the problems which were being experienced under actual field conditions. By the time the Camel was designed opposite-handed guns became available and it was then possible to tidy up the forward firing machine gun installation.

As the war developed it was obvious to the high command, from the massive build-up of German troops, that a major offensive was to take place before the Americans, who had now joined the war, could arrive in great numbers. It was certain that there would be further trench warfare so a request was made for a special ground-strafing aircraft. This was designated the EF Type No. 1 Armoured Trench Fighter.

The initial proposal was to arm a Camel with downward firing Lewis machine guns, adjustable between 35 and 55 degrees from the vertical, and armour plate the aircraft belly. A 110 hp Le Rhone engine was to be fitted, which was lighter than the Clerget, and would compensate somewhat for the weight of the armour plate. Sopwiths' designation for this was the TF1. It was decided therefore to secure three Camels and convert them for trials under service conditions.

There were certain complications involved in having the breeches and magazines of the Lewis guns in the already confined space in the cockpit. The forward firing armament was reduced to one Vickers gun. The armour plate was 8 mm thick and very heavy. Production requirements meant that the plate had to be cut out and drilled at Sopwith's factory and then returned to the Firth Steel Company for hardening. Because of the extra weight the wings needed strengthening. The aircraft proved to be heavy on the controls and tiring to fly, however it could be looped, rolled and spun without any difficulty. Enough was learned from this trial to lead to the design of the Salamander.

When the trench strafing Camels were returned from France after their trials it was pointed out that two forward firing guns, at a shallow angle of depression, covered a far greater killing area than a machine in level flight with acutely depressed guns.

With the demand for increased power and reliability, W.O. Bentley, who had been commissioned into the navy, was entrusted with the design of a new rotary engine. He began with what was known as the 150 hp AR1 (Admiralty Rotary) which was later renamed the BR1. His ideas for an improved engine worked and, after a few were produced, he was authorized to proceed with a larger engine to be known as the 230 hp BR2. It was the largest, and by far the most successful, of the rotary engines.

This engine incorporated some very important improvements. The cylinder barrels were of aluminium alloy with steel liners. This overcame the cylinder warping problems because of the much improved heat distribution. Having achieved this he was able to use aluminium alloy pistons with normal cast iron piston rings. The increase in power output was brought about by an increase in swept volume of the engine and increased efficiency. The engine finished up only 3 inches larger in diameter than the previous rotary engines that delivered 100 hp less.

With a powerful and reliable engine now available, Hawker was in a position to design an aircraft which was destined to become the replacement for the Camel as towards the end of 1917 there was an urgent need for a fighter having a better performance and fire power. In fact, it was to be a completely new aeroplane. By this time the system of choosing and ordering aircraft had become more formalized. A specification was prepared and issued by the Controller of the Technical Department of Aircraft Production at the Ministry of Munitions. It was for a single-seater fighter, designated A1a.

Nine types were submitted by various manufacturers, two of them from Sopwiths — the 7F1 Snipe and the 8F1 Snail. A process of elimination then took place lasting into 1918. Most of the submissions were rejected for various reasons, leaving four, three of which were powered by BR2 engines.

On 1 April 1918 the RFC and the RNAS ceased to exist and both were absorbed into the new separately administered Royal Air Force which then had a separate division known as the Naval Air Arm. (At this point the Admiralty lost control of aircraft development but continued to develop aircraft carriers, largely using adaptations of RAF aircraft. In 1939 this disastrous policy was reversed and the Admiralty again took control of the NAA which later became the Fleet Air Arm.)

This amalgamation resulted in the specification designations

A Sopwith TF 2 Salamander; box-like and rather ugly because of the weight of armour it carried.

The Sopwith One and a Half Strutter, armed with a single forward firing gun and a rear-mounted gun for the navigator.

A Sopwith 7 F1 Snipe. Note the radial engine, twin guns and shaped propeller.

A Sopwith F1 Camel. The most famous of the Sopwith fighters. Canvas hangars provide the backdrop.

being changed to meet the overall requirements. These designations were:

AF Type 1 Single seat Fighter (high altitude)
AF Type 11 Single seat Fighter (ground targets)

The three contenders for the original specification met the requirements of the AF Type 1 specification. By early March the three BR2 engined contenders, together with one other, the Armadillo were at Martlesham Heath aerodrome for evaluation. The tests were monitored closely to make sure the best possible aircraft was put into production as soon as possible.

Service pilots who had seen action were then called in to further evaluate the short list. One of these was Capt J.B. McCudden, who was the leading air ace at that time having shot down 57 enemy aeroplanes. The final choice was the Snipe, mainly due to its superior manoeuvrability.

The production line for Camels had been cleared and preparations were hurriedly made for manufacturing the Snipe.

Although Tom Sopwith, Sigrist and Hawker headed up the design and production team, a permanent design staff drafted out the working drawings and carried out the detail work. The short period of time that elapsed between the acceptance of the design in March and the delivery of aircraft in numbers to No. 43 Squadron RAF in September 1918 was remarkable. Barely 6 months after the new specification had been issued, the plane flew its first patrol.

The specification for the AF Type 11, to replace the TF2, was met by the Salamander which was derived from the Snipe. It was to have two forward firing Vickers guns, but depressed to a lower firing angle as the idea of an acutely angled downward firing gun had been abandoned.

The Salamander, due to the weight of armour, handled differently from the Snipe. It accelerated more quickly in a dive and much more use had to be made of the engine on final approach to control the rate of sink. However, it was quite manoeuvrable and the protection the armour gave was very appreciable as it was capable of stopping enemy armour-piercing bullets at a range of 150 feet. The side armour was also capable of deflecting bullets, provided it was at an angle of over 15 degrees from the perpendicular, and it generally gave very good protection against shrapnel from anti-aircraft fire. This plating brought about the most visible difference between the Salamander and the Snipe as the fuselage of the former was slab-sided, whereas the Snipe had a beautifully faired fuselage. Some improvements were made as experience was gained and these were rapidly put in hand.

(It is interesting to reflect, after years of designing more and more stability into fighters to provide a stable gun platform, the latest fighters have instability designed into them to the extent that it would be very difficult to fly them manually. Control is "fly by wire", when only computers and power controls can respond quickly enough to enable the aircraft to carry out many of the manoeuvres required in modern warfare, such as automatic weapon aiming and terrain following at very low levels to avoid radar detection.)

There are numerous records of Hawker visiting centres in both Britain and France. On one such visit to Villacoublay a British General came on the scene, full of his own importance and talking loudly about his opinion of the Sopwith Camel. He stated that he had a good deal of experience and had great difficulty getting them out of a spin.

In an undertone to a colleague Hawker said, "I don't believe he has ever flown one." He then ordered a two-seater Camel, which they happened to have, brought out from the sheds and invited the General to make a flight with him. Having climbed to about 2,000 feet he put the aeroplane into a spin from which he did not attempt to recover until the last moment. He then climbed up again and repeated the spin in the opposite direction. On landing the General made no comment, but stalked away, suddenly remembering he had important things to do elsewhere. The episode did not end there — Hawker was later asked, through official channels, for an apology.

Hawker usually flew himself across the Channel but on one occasion it was necessary for him to go over to Villacoublay by boat and train, a journey which to anyone, aviator or not, was a miserable proceeding during the war. It is said that he arrived at the aerodrome berating everything to do with the sea, the ships on it, the French railways, the railway officials, and anything connected with rail transport. Finally he explained that he must have a machine in which to fly back to England and not have to repeat the experience of his journey over.

For some time the French had been very short of aeroplanes, but his request was finally met, although with some difficulty. Sopwiths' representatives at Villacoublay applied to the Air Board to let them have a Camel for testing. The request was complied with and instructions were sent from London to the GHQ at Marquise for a Camel to be detached from stores and sent to Villacoublay. According to Hawker, a quaint old ruin turned up that had about as many flying properties as a tea tray. He was told that this was the only one available and its history was recounted in detail. Nothing daunted, he went out and had a look at it. After a few minutes' examination he expressed the opinion, rather cynically, that apparently it had some indication of it having once been an

(*Lower*) *Twin Vickers machine gun installed in a Sopwith Camel and firing through the propeller blades.*

(Upper) The upward firing mount for a forward firing Lewis machine gun. Note the Army insignia on the RFC officer's sleeve.

aeroplane, and he thought, with care, it might be flown to London. Anyhow after his trip out anything was better than boats and trains. He took the machine up and found it unsafe to fly in its existing condition. For one thing the engine very nearly fell from its mountings on landing.

As it happened there were one or two experimental Strutters, the property of the French Government, in the sheds. Hawker's standing was such that the officer in charge made the decision, in the interests of diplomacy, to order that the engine from one of these be removed and installed in the decrepit Camel.

Hawker set out for England in the Camel next morning in filthy weather. The staff at Villacoublay were worried about his safety as they could get no word of his arrival. It was some time before they received the welcome news that he had finally landed safely at his destination.

Really, they said, they had not the least anxiety, for they had unbounded confidence in what they described as Hawker's uncanny capacity for getting out of trouble. Nevertheless, there were considerable expressions of relief when news turned up that he had arrived. During the flight he had three forced landings owing to petrol feed failure caused by blockages from sundry odd bits of rubber tube in the fuel tank. How he ever got there was never discovered, but Hawker regarded it as all in the day's work.

Another story by a colleague of Hawker's, who was in charge of some of the work in France, gives a further insight into his nature.

They were converting the Sopwith Dolphins from the 200 hp ungeared Hispano Suiza engines to the latest and more powerful 300 hp Hispano Suiza engines. This was done on a workshop basis. A request was sent for Hawker to go across and generally see if the job was being done properly, as it was a major conversion. The greater weight of the engine meant a dramatic change in the balance of the aeroplane which had to be compensated. It also required different cowling. The Dolphins had a history of radiator and oil system problems with the 200 hp engines.

"It was an extremely important matter, not by any means solely from the point of view of Sopwiths but more from the point of view of the French and American armies in the field, who then had no fighting machines coming forward that could use the 300 hp Hispano Suiza engine.

"When Hawker arrived I pointed out to him that he must not be too particular, explaining to him the very serious situation. He did not hesitate a moment, but took the machine straight away into the air, and as there was some question as to its strength, now that the more powerful and heavier engine was fitted, he gave it a thorough good rolling, spinning and diving, just to make quite sure it was all right.

"It was so characteristic of the man in showing his complete

Starting up the Bentley BR2 engine in a Sopwith Snipe with the aid of a Hucks starter, mounted on a Model T car chassis.

absence of fear, even when there might be some doubt in his mind as to the capabilities of the machine. As a matter of fact when this machine was stressed it was found to be very seriously lacking, and before it was put into production it was strengthened.

"There is one other characteristic, little incident that occurred which illustrates his outspokenness when he knew an aeroplane was not right.

"I took him to the sheds of a very famous designer and constructor at Villacoublay to show him the new machine which had just been offered for test to the Technical Section of the French Government. It was supposed to be going to do all sorts of wonderful things.

"It was a weird affair, and its designer and constructor happened to be in the shed at the time. Hawker had a careful look over the whole machine and made one or two caustic comments to me. I then introduced him to the designer who was a fairly tall man, and Hawker, looking at him squarely with his brown eyes, enquired which way up the machine was intended to fly!

"It was a tense moment, but Hawker's obvious sincerity completely disarmed the Frenchman and they entered a long discussion about the design. Unfortunately I have no capacity for describing incidents of this sort, but it was really very comic, for it never occurred to Hawker that his remark may cause offence. The design was wrong, and that was all there was to it.

"I need hardly say he was correct in his views, as the machine never did anything except kill a couple of people, which was what Hawker said it would do.

"On another occasion there was a big four engined Bleriot being tested. Hawker was on the field when the machine crashed at its first flight. The pilot was, I believe, to be paid 1,000 francs for every minute he remained in the air. Hawker was aghast at the whole machine and that it should ever go into the air. He foretold precisely what would happen when it was flown.

"The tail twisted off and the machine, after falling like a stone, caught fire.

"Hawker's visits were very much looked forward to at Villacoublay, and amongst the French pilots he was a source of considerable admiration for the brilliancy of his work and his profound knowledge of air work generally. Everybody turned out when they got to know Hawker was in the air."

Chapter Eight

Marriage

The story of Hawker's meeting with his future wife and events leading up to their marriage can scarcely be better told than by the account of it in his wife's book.

"There must have been very few moments in Harry's life when he did not thoroughly enjoy himself and, since the time when I first met him in April 1915, stranded in a little light car which I used to drive in those days, his cheery optimism has helped him over disappointments and dangers which would have overcome a less buoyant nature. Some few incidents of the intimate side of his character help to show how he took life.

"One Sunday in April, while driving with a school friend through Richmond Park, we came to a sudden standstill halfway between the Kingston and Richmond Gates. Before starting that day I had seen that the boy had placed a spare tin of petrol in the back, and I had put this petrol into the tank before leaving Kingston. My knowledge of cars extended very little beyond the amount it took to get this particular light car along, so any stoppage was the source of much anxiety if it happened to occur far from the reach of assistance.

"I commenced to look for the trouble in the carburettor, but this seemed to be getting a proper supply of petrol. I dare not look so far afield as that mystery the magneto, and I began to look upon the person who could locate the cause of a stoppage almost immediately as a kind of wizard, there seemed so many things that might happen. While I turned the starting handle hoping that the car had forgotten its trouble, a Gregoire came by in which were two men, and it was a sign of awkward youth that I resolutely refused their proffered assistance, regretting it as soon as the car was out of sight.

"Presently I noticed the petrol dropping from the carburettor when I flooded her, instead of quickly disappearing into the ground, had accumulated into a puddle, and then the bright idea at last struck me that the tank had been filled up with nothing but water. I let all the contents of the tank out and resignedly settled down to wait for a passing car whose driver had a tin of petrol to spare. One or two passed, but we were unable to obtain petrol from them.

"Then the Gregoire returned, and this time pulled into the kerb. The driver, whom we were soon to know as Harry Hawker, got out

(Right) The Hawker home at Hook bedecked with bunting to celebrate Harry's safe return from his Atlantic adventure and near death.

and said, 'Was it petrol after all?' Rather surprised at this very lucky guess, we enquired as to how he got his knowledge. 'If a girl breaks down,' he said, 'she will invariably take everything down that is detachable before she looks into the petrol tank.' Although this was not quite fair in our case, it was characteristic of his almost uncanny gift of being able to discern what was wrong with a car almost without seeing it. I explained what had actually happened while Harry was filling our tank from his spare tin. We exchanged cards, or rather, it would have been an exchange had not Harry, after a lengthy search in many pockets, found he had left his case at home, and so wrote his name on the back of the other man's. He had a nervous, offhand manner all the time, and although he made one very unconvincing effort at a compliment on my knowledge of motor cars, he seemed genuinely relieved when I let in the clutch and with many thanks drove away.

"But this did not prove to be the end of the episode, for the following Sunday morning brought me a telephone message from the police. Vaguely wondering how I had broken the law, although when one drives a car one gets on quite a familiar footing with the police, I was surprised to hear that it was our rescuer of the previous Sunday who, with a sort of boyish enthusiasm, said he had bought a 27-80 hp Austro Daimler car during the week and suggested I should come and try it. So we four, newly made friends, set out and this was the

first time I drove a real motor car. It was characteristic of Harry's good nature that each car he had, and he had many during his lifetime, he was not only willing to let me drive, but pleased that I should want to drive it. Those who have a kind of love for their cars will know the effort required to let others handle them.

"Every Sunday during the summer we continued these drives without the knowledge of my parents, until these meetings were discovered, as such meetings usually are sooner or later. After a while I managed, by telling stories of his great gallantry, to persuade my mother, to ask Harry and his friend Basil, to dinner. After dinner my father and mother, and an old friend wished to get up a hand of whist, and Harry volunteered to make up the fourth, and sat down as though he enjoyed it.

"There were some young people there that night, and we all trooped off into another room to indulge in more enlivening pastimes. Whether he thought that to play a quiet game of cards with the older people would make a better impression than playing such childish games as we others were indulging in, is a debatable question, but I am not sure he would not have had more success had he joined us for, as I afterwards learned, he loathed cards, had played whist only once in his life before, and, needless to say, played a very bad game. However, his simple frankness found favour and we were allowed to continue our Sunday afternoon drives.

"Christmas drew near and mother, on finding that Harry and Basil would be alone in 'diggings' for the festive season, invited them to come and spend Christmas with us. 'Now, don't be late,' she admonished them as they said goodbye on the Sunday before. 'We have dinner at 4 o'clock on Christmas Day.' They certainly were not late, since they arrived at 4 o'clock on Christmas Eve, 24 hours before they were expected! Dad was the only one at home, and I arrived home at 6 o'clock to hear his recital of their brief call. I guessed at once they had made a mistake in the day, but Dad refused to agree with me.

"The incident was never mentioned to Harry until after we were married and about to spend Christmas in my old home. Then I said to Harry, as we were packing, 'We will not make a mistake in the day this time!', 'Good gracious!' exclaimed Harry, 'Do you mean to say my wonderful display of tact failed on that other occasion? As soon as we arrived, and I saw we were not expected, I guessed we were a day too soon.' He went on to tell me that he got out of a difficult situation by convincing Dad it was a time worn custom in Australia to make a call upon people the day before you went to stay with them. Then he thought of the tell tale bags in the back of the car. He fixed Basil with his eye, and in a meaning voice directed him to go out and turn off the petrol, as the joint leaked, and Basil took the tip. When Dad went out a little later to speed his two guests, the bags were hidden beneath a large fur rug. Now, Basil felt the cold intensely in England, but Harry not at all. So it must have been a study in expressions when, in answer to a suggestion from Dad that they should throw the rug over their knees, Harry assured him it was not necessary as neither of them felt the cold in the least!

"In those days of war, when Harry was very busy 7 days a week testing new machines, sometimes at the rate of 10 a day, and working half the nights on designs for new ones, it was brought home to me, on Harry's enquiry as to how I filled in my time, how little work I did to justify my existence. 'I bet you I will get some work within a fortnight', I told him and after arranging the nature of the bet, he took me on.

"Then followed a hunt for the elusive work. I had not the slightest idea where to begin, as I had no special qualifications. However, I applied at a Labour Exchange, an experience uncongenial in the extreme. I was asked to fill in some forms stating my qualifications and experiences. This did not take me long! I was then asked to fill in some more, and, after this, was told to go home and await their communication.

"In a few days I had a letter asking me to call on the Monday at the offices of the National Health Insurance Commission, Buckingham Gate. There were only 3 days more before the expiration of my bet with Harry, so I was only too glad to keep this appointment. I could have laughed aloud when Mr Alfred Woodgate, afterwards affectionately known as the Archangel, turned to his colleague Mr Bailey, under whom I afterwards worked, and observed, 'Let me see, Bailey, you are wanting someone at once, aren't you?' and I was told to consider myself engaged as from tomorrow. I wondered whether I ought to say, 'Thank you Mr Woodgate' or 'Thank you sir.' Eventually I just said, 'Thank you' and departed very elevated. Perhaps the greatest joys and sorrows of my life hung upon the words, 'Consider yourself engaged from tomorrow,' for that same evening Harry and I became provisionally engaged to be married. I say provisionally, because at that time, being still in my teens, and taking into consideration the uncertainties of war, I did not want to be tied completely.

"The Sunday rides were continued, generally to Brooklands, where there was always something for Harry to do. The Austro Daimler had been well hotted up and was now capable of 80 mph, and we spent many an exciting time strafing anything willing and able on the road. I often wonder what manner of curses we drew on our heads from nervous pedestrians who seem to enjoy ignoring the footpath and walking with their backs to traffic, or those 20 mile an hour motorists who love the very centre of the road and hate to move. I remember in particular an elderly gentleman walking slowly along the road by the side of which was a perfectly good and empty footpath, who, dropping his hat and stick, remained firmly planted on both feet and stared at us in open mouthed amazement and disapproval as we whizzed by. Certainly for his especial safety it would have been better had we indulged in our turn of speed on the footpath, But I am sure Harry was less of a danger on the road driving at 70 miles an hour than those, who cursed us most, driving at 20 or sauntering about in the middle of the fairway. These little trips did not cease, and I well remember the very last Sunday Harry was with me he said, 'Let's go out alone like we used to do and not take anyone with us.' We did so, but then we met some friends at tea time!

"I often wonder if the early days of our engagement would have been less stormy had I been more nearly Harry's intellectual equal or else a different type of girl altogether. But Harry had no time for the 'take care of me' kind of female, and I believe he thoroughly enjoyed our heated arguments. After we were married we drifted into an always interesting and exciting existence, and life was well worth living.

"We were married at St Peter's Church, Ealing, on 14 November 1917. Just before the appointed hour, I sent a message round to the church to see if Harry was there, as he so easily forgot the times of his engagements. But his brother, who was to attend him, had rounded him off the aerodrome at Brooklands, where he had completed the testing of a machine in the morning, and hustled him

The wedding of Harry Hawker and Muriel Peaty took place in London on 17 November 1917. Capt Bert Hawker, in the centre, was able to get leave from France to attend his brother's wedding.

into the awful clothes and awful hat customary at wedding ceremonies, which he wore for the first time. My first sane memory after the ceremony and reception were over was of a most appalling noise issuing from the room in which Harry was changing, and eventually some object was kicked into my room, which turned out to be the poor old hat in tatters!

"For months Harry had been saving petrol from all quarters, the restrictions on that commodity being very severe then, in order that we might spend our honeymoon on a motor tour. But motoring with petrol became quite prohibited, so Harry had a large stand built on the top of the Gregoire to hold a gas bag. We tried it a day or two before we were married and found we could run a matter of about 4 or 5 miles on the whole bag, which did not look very hopeful for a journey down to Cornwall. Anyway, we started with the gas bag up and the petrol tank full and a few extra tins of petrol in the back, since it was our intention to proceed by petrol except for an occasional mile or two by gas for appearances' sake. We filled up at Exeter, and arrived at Launceston the next day in time for lunch. A dear old waiter, very interested in us and our fearsome appendage, related for our benefit some incidents he remembered connected with the appearance of the first motorcar in Launceston. He asked us how far we could go with a bagful of gas. Harry said, 'Oh, 80 or 90 miles.' The waiter said someone had told him that gas bags were no good, as they could only do about 10 miles. But Harry informed him we carried compressed gas in an aluminium case, which assertion completely satisfied him and left him with the idea that he had just seen the last word in gas propelled vehicles! The gas bag was a nuisance, however, and we should have done just as well without it, despite the remark of the bobby inspecting petrol licences at Exeter. When he saw us coming out of the gas company's premises, he said with a grin, 'Ah! I see you have the laugh on the petrol restrictions!'

"All the horses shied at the wretched thing, and we were held up half an hour in a very narrow lane near Penzance owing to a horse which had shied, fallen, and refused to get up again through fear of our conveyance.

"It was at this period that Harry's back started to give trouble. A week or so before we were married he was flying a machine to France and had to make a forced landing into thick snow for some trivial cause. Not being able to speak any French to explain his presence there, and being in civilian clothes, he was taken into custody by the French authorities and placed in the guardroom. He was due to arrive at his destination Villacoublay, I think it was, before dark, so the delay was serious. He managed to get away on a passing English lorry, and with the assistance of two men he got the machine out of the snow and arrived at Villacoublay before dark. In moving the machine, he strained his back which, since his crash in

1913, was always apt to give trouble under a great strain. It did not get better, and a month later he went to bed for a time on his doctor's order. The treatment gave him no relief, so that after a fortnight he decided to get up and let his back cure itself which, for the time being, it did.

"He had no trouble of any description until 2 years later. One day, when he had been doing some heavy lifting in his work shop, he came in and complained once more of the pain in his back. It grew worse and worse, until he could not stoop or bend his back at all. He was then advised to consult a famous bone setter, who told him his trouble was an adhesion of muscles which would have to be broken away, an extremely painful process, but that when it was completed there would be no further trouble. Harry said, 'Go ahead', and every week he received the treatment and every week he seemed to get stiffer and to suffer more pain. He persevered with the treatment for some weeks, often in great pain, until I persuaded him to have further advice. He consulted a back specialist in London who, after having seen the X-ray photos of his back, gave the verdict that two courses only remained open to him. The first was to be flat on his back for 2 years; the second, an operation, by which new bone was to be grafted into the spine, followed by 12 months on his back. He was told that there was no alternative to these two remedies, as if his back were left in its present condition it would gradually grow worse until he could not move at all. Poor Harry! This was the greatest trial of his life.

"A few days later he was persuaded to have Christian Science treatment and, by a strange coincidence, Commander Grieve wrote to him on hearing of his trouble, telling him in his blunt way to give Christian Science a go. He told of cures that had been effected in the case of his own relatives, and said that he firmly believed that their lives were saved through Christian Science methods. Harry read out the letter, saying, 'Well, if it's good enough for old Mac, it's good enough for me!' He at once received the treatment and made a study of the Science. The result was magical. The pain in his back went away, not gradually, but immediately, and never to the end of his life, did he have any further trouble. Although his last year of life was filled with greater physical strain, during track racing, than any other year, he was able to bend his back, put on the weight which he had lost during the painful 2 months, and was his own cheery self again.

"I have written here just the bare truths of Harry's back trouble and cure, making no attempt to round it off with suggestions that the cure may have been the effect of his first adviser's treatment (just for the benefit of those sceptics who will smile) since it was his firm opinion that the Christian Science treatment did for him immediately and permanently, what no one, in whom these sceptics

144

Hawker with his wife Muriel and two daughters Pamela and Mary on the lawn at Hook.

An interesting historical photograph which shows Tom Sopwith (in background), Mackenzie Grieve and Hawker, with his wife Muriel, all in the same picture.

145

put their faith, could do. We all know so little and profess so much, and yet 99 out of 100 Christian people will back any guessing human doctor against their God, when bodily adjustments are necessary,and smile with amusement when the odd one seeks and receives his Maker's help.''

Chapter Nine

The Atlantic Crossing

In 1914, before World War I, a prize of 10,000 pounds was offered by the London *Daily Mail* for the first successful, nonstop crossing of the Atlantic Ocean. As a consequence of the outbreak of war this was not again considered until war ended in 1918. By this time aeroplanes were much improved, giving a much better chance of success and the *Daily Mail* renewed its offer.

The challenge was immediately taken up by Sopwiths and Hawker was the natural choice to take charge of the attempt and to carry out the modifications to one of their aeroplanes to give it the extra range needed. He would, of course, also pilot the aircraft. He chose as navigator a man he had met when he was involved with deck landing trials on HMS *Campania*, Lt Cdr K.K. Mackenzie Grieve. When he was selected as navigator he went, at his own request, to Eastchurch and qualified for his pilot's licence in 6 days.

The aircraft was a specially adapted modification of the Sopwith B1 and was christened the *Atlantic*. The fuselage depth was increased to accommodate the large fuel tanks required. The rear fairing, behind the cockpits, was constructed in the form of a boat, made from plywood, which could be removed and used as a lifeboat in case of a forced landing in the sea The aircraft wings were modified to give a larger area to support the considerable load. The wingspan was 46 feet and the wing area 575 square feet.

Hawker decided that it would be a great advantage if the undercarriage could be dropped after take-off. It would reduce the drag and weight considerably and consequently increase the range of the aeroplane. He considered that if they did have to come down in the sea they would be much better off without it as the aircraft would not be so likely to go over on its nose. The undercarriage had to be strengthened considerably to take the increased load of fuel and equipment, with a consequent heavy weight penalty, so a release gear was designed and fitted. The drag of the undercarriage was found to be significant and when it was released after departure from Newfoundland the airspeed increased by 7 mph.

A 12 cylinder, V type, water-cooled Rolls-Royce Eagle Eight engine of 360 hp was fitted. At cruising speed the fuel consumption of this

(Right) An interesting annotated photo of the Atlantic *published in a contemporary magazine.*

engine was 15 gallons per hour. A tank capacity of 330 gallons was provided to give an endurance of 22 hours which should have been just about enough, with a small reserve, for the 2,000 mile flight at the cruising speed of 105 mph which gave a total flight time of just over 19 hours, if all went well. With extra oil the total all up weight on take-off was 6,150 lbs.

All this modification and reconstruction was carried out in the brief period of 6 weeks. A test flight with the fuel tanks three-quarters full was carried out satisfactorily. A radio was fitted, but difficulties were experienced and it was not used on the flight.

The aircraft was then boxed up in a strong crate, which later proved to be necessary with all the transshipping that was required to get it to the field. Some of the difficulties they encountered are well illustrated in the accompanying photographs.

An insight into Hawker's nature is revealed in this extract from his wife's book:

"...they went steadily forward with their preparations and were eventually ready to start for St Johns, Newfoundland on 28 March 1919. Harry and Cdr Grieve, in a preliminary test at Brooklands, in

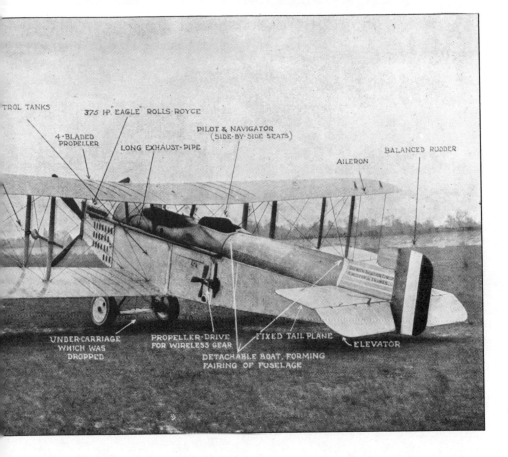

TROL TANKS
4-BLADED PROPELLER
375 H.P. EAGLE ROLLS-ROYCE
LONG EXHAUST-PIPE
PILOT & NAVIGATOR (SIDE-BY-SIDE SEATS)
AILERON
BALANCED RUDDER
UNDER-CARRIAGE WHICH WAS DROPPED
PROPELLER-DRIVE FOR WIRELESS GEAR
FIXED TAIL PLANE
DETACHABLE BOAT, FORMING FAIRING OF FUSELAGE
ELEVATOR

one day, flew a distance of 1,800 miles, equivalent to the Atlantic flight, and there was no hitch, not even in the sandwiches I cut for them!

"Jury's Imperial Pictures produced a film showing Harry's trials for the Atlantic flight conducted at Brooklands prior to his leaving for Newfoundland. The operator who took this film went up in a second machine when Harry was in the air.

"It was pouring with rain the day Harry started, and bitterly cold. During the preparations my courage had remained high, but when I went into Harry's room just before we left, and found him crying, I lost heart and broke down entirely. He had been putting a last few things into his bag, when his feeling got the better of him. He was always sensitive and softhearted, and I knew he was going to be terribly homesick until he got over the other side and had plenty to do. The sight of his grief was too much for me, and my courage oozed out altogether. But tears, even the tears of a grown-up man and woman, are a wonderful relief to overwrought feelings. We felt much better afterwards and were able to look on the bright side of things once more.

The four transatlantic fliers just prior to their attempt to cross the Atlantic Ocean. From left to right: Mackenzie Grieve, Raynham, Hawker and Morgan.

"I only went as far as London to see Harry off, for I could not leave our baby for long at a time. The drive could hardly be described as cheerful. I sat on the floor of the 12 cylinder Sunbeam, for better protection from the rain, as we carried no hood. With my head on Harry's knee, I longed to sleep away the next 2 months. He reached the station only just in time to catch the train, and a number of friends had gathered to see him off. I recall that, at that moment, I wished I had married a farmer's lad with no ambitions. I was thankful when the whistle blew, as I felt so very unsure of myself and was afraid of breaking down again. He was gone, and all I could do was to wait for the future to unfold itself.

"I got back home at 10 o'clock in the morning, oppressed by a feeling of great desolation. I could not settle to anything, and even Pam could not brighten me up.

"After the first week of Harry's absence, time at home went fairly quickly. I never left home for longer than 2 hours, and when I did I bought newspapers of every edition, in the hope of getting news."

The party, including a Rolls-Royce engine expert, set off aboard the SS *Digby* with the *Atlantic* safely stowed in the hold. It had, fortunately, been securely boxed as it had a rather hazardous journey, first by rail and then road, from its landing place at Placentia Bay in Newfoundland on 28 March, to the place of departure near St Johns. The original plan to take the aeroplane off the boat at St Johns was thwarted because the harbour was icebound.

Capt Montague Fenn, who had been in charge of the Paris office of Sopwiths, had led an advance party over to secure a suitable field for departure and make the necessary arrangements for fuel etc. The fact that the whole place was under snow did not make their task easy. The nature of the topography made it extremely difficult to find a good field from which to operate. They finally selected a site and proceeded to build a wooden shed in which to erect the aircraft which would provide some protection from the weather. The best field they could find was very rough which was going to make the take-off very difficult, and not without risks as it could not be used in all wind directions.

The aircraft was transported from the railhead at St Johns to the field, by means of horse drawn waggons, which frequently bogged in the mud on the unmade roads. It was finally unpacked and the various parts carried into the hangar where the wings were put on and the whole aircraft rigged. Because the ground was so uneven, testing was limited to one test flight with a light load under favourable wind conditions.

They were to undergo a most frustrating wait with bad weather persisting right up until the time they actually departed. A new radio was secured but they were unable to test it. About all they could do was start the engine from time to time and recheck everything.

(Upper left) Trans-shipping the Atlantic *aeroplane from the* SS Digby *to the* Portia *in Placentia Bay on its arrival in Newfoundland.*

(Lower left) Landing the container that held the Atlantic *onto a rail car at the wharf in St Johns.*

(Upper) A graphic picture that shows the state of the roads over which the Atlantic *had to be transported after it left the railhead.*

Because of the cold weather this meant filling and draining the radiator each time, which Hawker later thought could have led to the overheating problems he experienced as it would have encouraged the formation of sediment. This is somewhat doubtful as a thorough examination of the cooling system, after the aeroplane was recovered, found no traces of residue.

They carried with them insulated rubber suits, with air bags back and front which could be inflated for flotation. During the time they were waiting for the weather to improve they were able to test these out, together with the boat which formed the fairing behind the cockpits.

While all this was going on another contender for the *Daily Mail* prize had arrived in St Johns on 10 April. This was a Martynside aeroplane crewed by Raynham and Morgan. Raynham was an old rival who had competed in the British Duration Record and in many other races. The field that had been selected by Raynham allowed for take-off in only one direction and was even worse than the one Hawker was going to use.

Both parties were staying in St Johns. They had always been the best of friends and remained so, although there was a cat and mouse game to see who would be first off. Hawker relates that they indulged in plenty of practical jokes to liven up the time and visited the meteorological station together to get the latest information on the weather.

As tension built up, both parties arrived at a simple agreement that they would give each other 2 hours' notice of any decision to start. This relieved the pressure considerably, and both agreed that what really was at stake was the prestige of British aviation. There was also the thought that they might be able to provide help should one or the other have trouble.

When Raynham was asked what safety precautions he had taken, he replied that he proposed to "Fly the Atlantic, not fall into it." In the event Raynham and Morgan crashed while taking off but, fortunately, were not hurt.

"The weather was uniformly rotten," according to Hawker's account. "Sometimes the weather would clear up a bit and look promising, but the reports from the meteorological station almost always continued to put a different complexion on it. The thick white fogs would, whenever the wind went into the east, roll in from the banks and make flying impossible. We sometimes felt like having a go in spite of the bad weather but the aerodrome was not the sort of ground one could negotiate in those conditions."

About this time three American seaplanes arrived at Trespassy, which was also in Newfoundland, to commence a transatlantic flight, but were similarly held back by the weather. They planned to track by way of the Azores where they had fuel supplies and the US Navy

(Upper) This photo gives some idea of the size of the Atlantic. Workers are probably priming the engine by turning the propeller.

(Lower) This photo also gives some idea of the size of the Atlantic.

Testing the detachable fuselage fairing in its role as a lifeboat on a lake in Newfoundland. The life-saving suits were tested here also.

The detachable fuselage fairing of the Atlantic *which was designed to double as a lifeboat.*

had ships strung out along their proposed route in case they needed assistance. They were not eligible for the *Daily Mail* prize which was for a nonstop flight. However, their track would take them into improving weather as it was more southerly.

The direct route Hawker planned was more northerly due to fuel range requirements and, consequently, they could expect worse weather. This development restored some of the tension, because a matter of national pride dictated that the British fliers make the Atlantic crossing first, even though the Americans were not attempting the crossing on a nonstop basis.

On Sunday 18 May the weather reports seemed to be more favourable, or perhaps the sense of urgency that now existed coloured their judgement. The decision was made to depart that day and the *Atlantic* was made ready, tanks and Thermos flasks filled and everything aboard. The engine started and warmed up for take-off at 5.42 pm on 18 May. (They apparently left Newfoundland in the early afternoon so that they would have a number of daylight hours of flying before nightfall.) The take-off was accomplished safely but with little runway to spare. The engine was performing well and, after the coast was passed, the undercarriage release was pulled and it dropped away safely. This reduced the load and the air resistance which improved the climb, and the speed performance by 7 mph.

The undercarriage was subsequently recovered from the sea. When it was dropped sea currents carried it around the south coast of the Avalon Peninsula and up into Placentia Bay, where it was discovered and retrieved by a fisherman. It was then sent to St Johns railway and then taken to the dockside where it was put on display, at which time the photograph shown on page 173 was taken. It was then presented to the Newfoundland Museum, where it remained on display for the next 15 years.

In 1934 the Government took over the building in which the Museum was housed and converted it to Government offices. The Museum collection was placed in storage at a variety of locations. When the Museum was re-established in 1950 there was no sign of the *Atlantic's* undercarriage. The remains, which had deteriorated during storage, subsequently turned up and the one surviving wheel is now at the Museum workshop at St Johns.

The actual flight has been covered, in Hawker's own words, in the Prologue but a few further details are available from other sources. It is clear that the weather was appalling and one cannot help but be lost in admiration of their magnificent airmanship.

They were able to navigate and fly the aeroplane against all odds. One has to remember that their flight instruments were of the most basic kind. They had only a compass which, in rough air, swung all over the place making it difficult to maintain any kind of accurate course, and for determining the attitude of the aeroplane a crude turn and bank indicator together with an air speed indicator and an altimeter.

That they were able to fly through such foul weather, and survive, can only be properly appreciated by anyone who has done any instrument flying. No stabilized gyro instruments or automatic pilots in those days! The strain of continual hand flying, without any hope of relief for at least 24 hours, was a daunting prospect. All this, in an open cockpit in near freezing, wet weather, would have been attended by the most severe physical discomfort and accompanied by the continual noise from the engine. Superimpose on this the clear thinking required to handle the problems encountered when the cooling system began to boil and the sheer determination of these men becomes apparent.

They had to try and maintain a reasonable course, in spite of the navigation problems caused by their inability to take reliable sights or to get any idea of the drift from the wind which, as they progressed, would undoubtedly change in both direction and speed. Hawker had to handle it all with the growing realization that a ditching in mid-Atlantic was becoming inevitable. The possibility that they would emerge from such foul weather within sight of a ship would have been almost too slim to contemplate.

They finally reached the point where they could not possibly continue the flight and were faced with ditching the aircraft. After emerging through the low cloud they were able to fly around for a short while, hoping to sight a ship.

To their unbounded joy the impossible happened, a ship loomed up out of the murk! Their shouts of elation were blown away by the wind, and the serious business of ditching the *Atlantic* close to the ship occupied their whole attention. Much to their relief and delight they were able to attract the attention of the crew of the ship, which turned out to be the *Mary*.

After ditching alongside the *Mary*, which in itself must have been a must hazardous exercise, the *Atlantic* remained afloat because the tanks were, by then, about half empty and would have provided sufficient buoyancy to keep the plane afloat until such time as it started to break up. Waves, up to 12 feet high from the heavy sea that was running, were breaking over the aeroplane, which was almost awash. They were able to remain with the aircraft, however, and the first thing they did was to free the emergency boat which was done without any difficulty and, for the time being, left tethered to the aeroplane. The survival suits worked well and kept them dry and warm, which was just as well as it was an hour and a half before the lifeboat from the *Mary* could reach them in the rough conditions.

When they ditched alongside the *Mary* the water temperature must have been very low as they were then at a more northerly

A drawing by an American artist of Hawker and Grieve in their waterproof life-saving suits.

latitude than their point of departure, and they reported seeing numerous icebergs after crossing the coast of Newfoundland.

When they finally got on board the *Mary* they found the position where they had come down was 49 deg 47 min N, 29 deg 7 min W. The distance covered was about 1,050 miles. The elapsed time from departure to being picked up from the sea was about 14 hours 30 minutes. They were about halfway across the Atlantic and had more than enough fuel to complete the trip, had they not had trouble with the weather and the cooling system.

The question of salvaging the *Atlantic* was discussed with Capt Duhn after boarding the *Mary*, but it was decided that it was not possible because of the rough seas running at the time. Reluctantly it had to be abandoned to the mercies of the Atlantic Ocean, thankful that they at least had been saved.

Having being provided with dry clothing they were too exhausted from their exposure and effort to eat, and retired to the ship's bunks for a well earned sleep. In addition to being under considerable stress from the weather, and the problems they encountered, they had both suffered air and then seasickness. After a good rest and a welcome hot meal there was not much to be done but await their landfall, which was delayed because of continuing foul weather.

Unfortunately the *Mary* did not carry a radio so they were unable to let the outside world, and their families, know that they had been rescued. This would have been frustrating as both men knew faint hope would have been held for their survival after so long a time.

Meanwhile, back in England hope faded that they would ever be seen again.

On 24 May Muriel Hawker received a telegram from the King:

"The King; fearing the worst must now be realised regarding the fate of your husband, wishes to express his deep sympathy, and that of the Queen, in your sudden and tragic sorrow. His Majesty feels the Nation lost one of its most able and daring pilots who sacrificed his life for the fame and honour of British flying."

In spite of this, and the constant press reports that all hopes were gone, Muriel retained her faith that somehow Harry would turn up. Muriel Hawker's faith was rewarded because on 26 May, the day following receipt of the telegram from the King and just one week after they had departed from Newfoundland, word came through that they had been picked up by the *Mary*. The joy and relief were indescribable. When the news was confirmed another telegram arrived from the King:

"The King rejoices with you, and the Nation, on the happy rescue of your gallant husband. He trusts that he may be long spared to you."

Off the coast of Scotland they were picked up from the *Mary* by the British destroyer HMS *Woolston* and transferred to Admiral

Fremantle's Flagship, HMS *Revenge*. They were landed at Thurso the next morning and began their triumphal journey back to London.

The nature of their reception can only be described as that of heroes. The whole thing had captured the imagination of the population and cheering crowds welcomed them everywhere. Although they had failed in their attempt to cross the Atlantic Ocean, through no fault of their own, they had demonstrated great courage and determination, and had returned from the dead. The collective relief was shown in no uncertain manner throughout their journey from Thurso, and the aviators arrived back in London on Tuesday evening, 27 May 1919.

A telegram was awaiting them from the King, commanding them to attend at Buckingham Palace at 10.30 the following morning. When they arrived they were received by the King, who congratulated them and honoured each of them with the award of the Air Force Cross. The ceremony was followed by many questions about the flight. His Majesty was deeply interested in the first hand account of their experiences.

Hawker and Grieve were feted and inundated with all forms of expression of congratulation and good will. At one function, in proposing the toast to "two very gallant gentlemen", General Seely summed up everyone's feelings:

"...they have rightly had a welcome, they filled our hearts with joy because there was a happy ending to this glorious adventure with such possibilities in the future. They dared, and did a great thing, but in our hearts we all rejoice, Mrs Hawker, that your husband was brought back to you from the jaws of death.

"On behalf of the Air Ministry I am privileged to hand you this scrap of paper. It is a very real scrap of paper. It contains, not only a generous gift from a man (Lord Northcliffe) to whom the whole of aviation owes so much, and whom we hope shortly to see restored to health, but is also an emblem of the thoughts of your countrymen for a gallant deed done for the honour of your country. I congratulate you, Mr Hawker and Cdr Grieve."

The "scrap of paper" was a cheque for 5,000 pounds from the *Daily Mail* in recognition of their performance, in spite of the fact that they were unsuccessful in being able to claim the prize for the nonstop crossing.

By an extraordinary stroke of luck the wreckage of the *Atlantic* was sighted in the middle of the vast expanse of the Atlantic by the crew of the SS *Lake Charlotteville* on 23 May, they hauled it out of the water and landed it at Falmouth, 5 days later on 28 May.

The reported position where it had been picked up was only seven nautical miles from where it had been abandoned. It had settled further into the water leaving only the tail and the rear part of the fuselage projecting vertically above the water.

Muriel Hawker being congratulated by her brother Capt Peaty
and her sister who holds baby Pamela.

Capt Mackenzie Grieve and his wife read the news of their son's rescue.

It must be remembered that the position where the *Mary* picked up Hawker and Grieve could not have been known by the Captain of the *Lake Charlotteville*, because the *Mary* had no wireless. The most they could have known was that the aeroplane had not arrived at its destination and could have been anywhere across the Atlantic. This is another incident in a most extraordinary chain of events. The vigilance of the crew of the ship in sighting the floating derelict must have been very keen.

There was a heavy swell running when the *Lake Charlotteville* approached the *Atlantic*. Not knowing that the airmen had been rescued, they spent some time searching for survivors. The aeroplane was not badly damaged when it was picked up having, remarkably, survived the battering from the rough seas. It was carefully hoisted on deck by winches but later a large wave swept the deck causing further damage. It therefore arrived in Falmouth somewhat the worse for wear.

"The steamer arrived at Falmouth at 4 pm on 28 May, with the remains of the aeroplane lashed on to the deck, looking at a distance like a broken perambulator. Although the engine did not appear to have suffered a great deal from the effects of immersion, the aluminium was noticeably corroded. The propeller was smashed and splintered, as also was the timber structure of the machine. There was a mass of twisted wires among the fractured wings and soaked canvas."

The Captain of the *Lake Charlotteville*, Cdr Wilvers, followed the usual practice for property salvaged at sea and handed the wreckage to the Receiver of Wrecks, claiming salvage rights.

Representatives of the *Daily Mail*, Sopwiths and Selfridges (the big London store) travelled by early train the following morning to discuss the possible purchase of the remains. This was negotiated and the remains were brought ashore and transported to London where it was displayed on Selfridge's roof in Oxford St. There had been so much public interest aroused by the popular heroes that thousands of people visited the remains of their aeroplane.

Hawker was naturally delighted when he heard the machine had been picked up.

"Its recovery will be of the greatest value," he said, "for on it are many records which will be of the greatest value to the science of aviation. In addition there is a quantity of mail, which happily will not be very much damaged by the water, as it is in waterproof containers. Some of the instruments are of delicate construction and these, we hope, will give valuable information for future flights."

When the welcoming festivities were over, Hawker and his wife decided to get away for a well earned rest and a holiday on their own after the strains and excitement of the preceding 2 months. They went to stay in a little seaside place in Norfolk where they hoped they

Where the Airmen were Picked Up

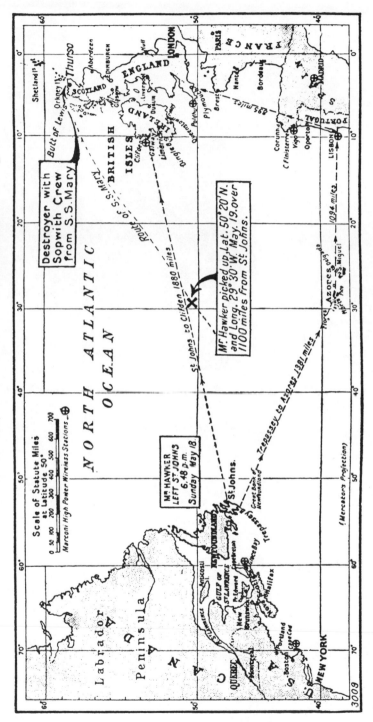

The cross shows the spot where Hawker and Grieve were rescued by the SS Mary, which then proceeded on her course to Denmark, past the Butt of Lewis, until she was intercepted by the British destroyer Woolston.

(Upper) The derelict Atlantic *floating tail up was found in mid Atlantic by the* SS Lake Charlotteville — *a remarkable photograph.*

(Upper right) The wreckage of the Atlantic *on the deck of the* SS Lake Charlotteville *on its arrival at Falmouth.*

(Lower right) The remains of the Atlantic *being lifted onto the wharf at Falmouth.*

(Upper left) Hawker and Mackenzie Grieve leaving Buckingham Palace in a Rolls-Royce after being decorated by the King. Although a civilian, Hawker received a Service Decoration — the Air Force Cross.

(Lower left) When Hawker and Mackenzie Grieve arrived at Kings Cross Station a tumultuous welcome awaited them. Large numbers of Australian servicemen due for repatriation were in the crowd.

(Upper) Hawker, riding a police horse, proudly carries an Australian flag on his way to the Aero Club.

The remains of the Atlantic *were displayed on the roof top of Selfridges store in Oxford Street, London.*

The wreckage of the Atlantic *being hoisted onto the roof of Selfridges.*

would not be recognized. This was too much to hope or expect.

They had some very welcome peace and quiet for the first day or two but, such was Hawker's fame, people soon became aware of their identity. On the second day, after returning from a pleasant morning walk, they were met with many interested looks and a small child appeared with an autograph book. This really let the cat out of the bag and by tea time the whole village turned up with autograph books.

To get some of the peace and quiet they so badly needed they moved on to Cromer but, again, Harry's popularity soon gave them away and they were besieged by crowds of people, and again they moved. They were driving the Sunbeam car which probably helped to identify them. The only alternative then was to make it into a touring holiday, staying just one night at each place, hoping to keep one step ahead of the crowds.

One sad sequel to the rescue occurred when it was reported during the early part of World War II that the Danish vessel, the *Mary* was torpedoed and sunk off the coast of Brittany.

The probable reason for the overheating problems that forced them to land in the sea can now be better evaluated. At the time Hawker was of the opinion that sediment and solder particles had partially blocked the water pump intake. However, after the aeroplane was salvaged from the sea and later examined, no material could be found in the cooling system that could have caused any blockage. It is now thought most likely that the radiator itself had frozen and caused the restriction to the flow of the cooling water. Considering the weather they encountered, and the low temperatures experienced at the higher altitudes, this would not be surprising. The descent to lower levels, into warmer air, probably resulted in a thawing of the ice in the radiator which brought about the resumption of water circulation and the drop in cooling system temperatures reported.

The author's experience suggests that they were confronted with another problem about which very little was known at that time, and that was carburettor icing. The description of the difficulty they had in restarting the engine after one descent is a typical result of this phenomenon which is now quite well known with aeroplane engines equipped with carburettors. These are now invariably fitted with a carburettor air intake through which hot air can be induced from a muff which surrounds part of the exhaust system.

It is standard practise to apply heat to the carburettor at intervals whenever the throttle is closed, or partly closed, on descent to guard against engine failure. They were indeed lucky that the ice melted, when they encountered a warmer stratum of air, in time for them to restart the engine before contact with the sea.

Carburettor icing is most likely to occur at ambient air

(Left) Dropping the detachable undercarriage into St Johns Harbour shortly after take-off. It was later recovered.

(Lower) The undercarriage of the Atlantic *on the wharf at St Johns after being retrieved by a fisherman.*

temperatures just above freezing point, when the air contains a substantial amount of moisture. It is brought about by a temperature drop which occurs when the latent heat of the atomising fuel drops the temperature of the air to below freezing point. When the moisture laden air/fuel mixture encounters any obstruction, such as the throttle butterfly valve, the moisture freezes and ice formation occurs. This can take place quite rapidly and can quickly restrict the air supply to the engine with a resultant loss of power. If allowed to continue it can build up sufficiently to cause complete engine failure.

This problem is reinforced by the fact that, 2 weeks later, when Alcock and Brown did make the Atlantic crossing in the twin engine Vickers Vimy, Brown had to get out on the wings and chip the ice deposits off the outside of the carburettors. In this case the internal icing was not catastrophic because they were maintaining level flight and not making descents at low throttle openings. It does demonstrate, however, that below certain temperatures with the presence of moisture, significant ice deposition can occur.

It must be borne in mind that Alcock and Brown were nearing the end of their flight before they encountered icing conditions. Their fuel load by this time would have been very low and less power would have been required to maintain level flight.

Carburettor icing was not, at that time, recognised as a problem and it was not until later that any provision for coping with it was introduced. The engines of that time had no provision for heating induction air before it reached the carburettor. The water-cooled engines usually had water-jacketed intake manifolds between the carburettor and the engine. These were provided as a matter of engine efficiency and had nothing to do with preventing build up of ice in the carburettor.

This matter has been dealt with at length to emphasise that these early aviators were sometimes facing hazards, the full extent of which were not recognized at that time.

MR. HAWKER'S OWN STORY.

WHY THE MACHINE CAME DOWN.

TO-DAY'S WELCOME IN LONDON.

THE KING'S MESSAGE.

Mr. Hawker and Commander Mackenzie-Grieve's own accounts of the flight are printed below. The defect in the pipe which eventually caused the airmen to abandon the flight and to change their course in the happily successful attempt to meet a ship first showed itself after they had been flying for some five hours. Conquered at first, the defect recurred and compelled them to come down.

As was anticipated, the airmen struck very heavy weather in mid-Atlantic, and it was a matter of some time and considerable difficulty and danger before they were able to win to safety on the Mary.

The King has telegraphed inviting Mr. Hawker to Buckingham Palace to-morrow.

The King in a warm message to Mrs. Hawker heads the long list of messages of rejoicing and congratulation which have come from all quarters of the earth.

The stedfast confidence of Mrs. Hawker—a confidence which almost bears the mark of inspiration—was referred to in *The Times* yesterday. We print to-day letters she wrote to Lord Northcliffe and the Editor of the *Daily Mail* in the dark days last week, when the hopes of most people had vanished. These letters breathe a spirit of unwavering optimism and hope.

An account of some of the difficulties of aerial navigation which Commander Mackenzie-Grieve had to surmount is printed, together with further particulars of the navigator's career.

London will give an enthusiastic welcome to the airmen when they arrive at King's Cross at 7 o'clock this evening. After a civic welcome at the station, a procession will be formed, and an Australian military escort will accompany the airmen to the Royal Aero Club.

THE AIRMEN ON THE FLIGHT.

HEAVY STORM AND DENSE CLOUDS.

(FROM OUR SPECIAL CORRESPONDENT.)

INVERNESS, MAY 26.

Mr. Harry Hawker and Commander Mackenzie-Grieve, R.N., arrived at Thurso from H.M.S. Revenge this morning, and had a great municipal welcome. They have since made a triumphal progress through the Highlands *en route* to London.

At every little Highland station they were cheered, and men clung to the moving train.

In minutes between Mr. Hawker gave me his plain tale of adventure.

"Everything," he said, "went well at the start.

"We had a very difficult ground to rise from on the other side. To get in the air at all we had to run diagonally across the course.

"Once we got away we climbed very well, but about 10 minutes up we passed from firm, clear weather into the fog of the Newfoundland Banks. We got well over this, however, and, of course, at once lost sight of the sea.

"The sky was quite clear for the first four hours, when the visibility became very bad. Heavy cloud banks were encountered, and eventually we flew into a heavy storm with rain squalls.

"Trouble did not begin until we were five and a half hours out from St. Johns. Then the temperature of the water in the radiator began to rise. That did not mean a great deal at that moment, but we could see that something was the matter with the water circulation.

"It was part of my job to watch. Grieve was busy taking sights. It was about 11 p.m. Greenwich (midnight, summer time), and the clouds were exceptionally thick. We had not seen the water since we were ten minutes out from St. Johns.

"Our height was about 10,000 feet, and there were many cloud peaks up to 15,000, making a very bad horizon ; there being no moon, it not having risen by then and having to go round the clouds, it was difficult to steer a good course.

CAUSE OF THE TROUBLE.

" We were very comfortable—not cold a bit. but it was freezing hard. On we went, and the water temperature in the radiator rose from 168deg. to 176 (212 is boiling point) in a few minutes, and maintained that for a couple of hours or more.

" We were now looking for a cause and I came to the conclusion that something had got into the water filter between the radiator and water pumps, and the only thing we could do was to stop the motor, put the nose of the machine down steeply, with the hope that this would clear the refuse in the filter, and this was successful.

" But it was again choked in the next hour, and this brought us to about 800 miles out. The weather was still very bad, and the clouds very high, and several times we tried to clear, but unsuccessfully, and doing this meant losing height at every attempt. Each time after climbing the water boiled badly. That meant wasting water (i.e., the water for cooling the engine), and after getting to 12,000ft. again we decided to stop at this height for the rest of the way.

" We had not yet doubted being successful in getting across. We were then above most of the clouds. The moon was up, and we were keeping a good course, although we had to close the throttle and go a little slower to keep the water temperature below boiling point.

DENSE BLACK CLOUDS.

" We continued on this until twelve and a half hours out. Then we came to clouds again, very, very high, I should say about 15,000ft., very black, too, almost impossible to fly through. Each time we tried to climb above them we boiled badly.

" So I decided to go beneath them. Coming down to about 6,000ft. we found it blacker than ever. Eventually I got to 1,000ft. above the water before we could see to fly.

" We started on our course again with the sun just getting up, but could not keep the temperature below boiling.

" Then it was we reached the fateful decision to play for safety. We decided to fly diagonally south-east and then south-west across our course to see if we could find a ship, for we knew we could not go on indefinitely boiling our water away.

" This we did for about two and a half hours before we found a ship, the sea being very rough below, and we getting knocked about very badly at times. The wind was blowing from the north-east at half a gale.

A SHIP SIGHTED.

" At last I sighted a ship close to us on our port (left) bow. We were both fairly in the fog, with the clouds low, and we were almost on the top of her before we saw her.

" We flew alongside her at 400ft., fired three Very distress signals, and waited some time, flying across and across until she got some men up on deck.

" Then we went ahead about two miles and landed in front of her. We made a very good landing, although a very high sea was running and the machine floated on an even keel well out of the water.

" 'And that's that,' we said, and watched the steamer approaching. We put our own boat out, and stood by in case the machine should break up and sink, which it began to do rapidly in a heavy sea. The sea was running up 12ft. and breaking right over the machine and us.

" Our life-saving suits kept us dry, and for an hour and a half we watched the crew trying to launch a lifeboat. She was only 200 yards away. After much difficulty she succeeded in getting to us, and we boarded the lifeboat and were pulled to the ship by a line.

" Owing to the heavy sea it was impossible to salve anything at all. When we got to the ship we were without boots or caps, and Grieve without a coat. We were very sorry to lose a lot of valuable instruments and mail.

14½ HOURS OUT.

" Altogether before being picked up we had been 14½ hours out from Newfoundland. We were picked up at 8.30 a.m. on Monday, Greenwich time (9.30 British summer time).

" On climbing aboard we found that Captain Duhn spoke very good English. He had been afraid we should go down before his boat reached us. 'Another hour,' he said as we went on the bridge, 'and you would have gone down.' He thought we were Americans, and we were struck by the casual manner in which he took the whole business, as if it were an everyday affair to take airmen out of the Atlantic.

" We immediately asked him his bearings and what likelihood there was of meeting a ship that day or the next and being in the main route of shipping. At that time he thought there would be a very good chance of seeing a ship with wireless at any moment.

" That night the storm got worse and he had to heave to, only making about a knot in a northerly direction, this taking us off the shipping route and lessening the chance of meeting another ship.

HOW THE VOYAGE WAS PASSED.

" We slept or tried to most of the time, drank tea, and read the captain's English books. We saw St. Kilda, but it was not until the Butt of Lewis that we could communicate.

" Off Loch Erribol we were met by the destroyer Woolston and conveyed to Scapa Flow, where we had a splendid welcome home from Admiral Fremantle and the men of the Grand Fleet.

" What we want to emphasize is that the fault was not due to the motor, which was in every way reliable, running satisfactorily from start to finish ; even after boiling all the water away the motor was still running merrily, though red hot when we alighted in the water."

WELCOME HOME.

TO-DAY'S TRIUMPHAL PROCESSION.

AUSTRALIAN MILITARY ESCORT.

Mr. Hawker and Commander Mackenzie-Grieve are due to arrive at King's-cross this evening at 7 o'clock. They will travel from Grantham accompanied by Mrs. Hawker and Mr. and Mrs. Sopwith, who leave King's Cross by the 11.40 train this morning. An organized reception, civic and military, has been arranged. The mayor of St. Pancras with the aldermen and councillors, will greet the airmen on behalf of the borough of St. Pancras as they set foot within the borough boundaries.

A procession will then be formed. The airmen will proceed in motor-cars to the Royal Aero Club, preceded by an Australian military band specially ordered from Salisbury for the occasion, and escorted by Australian soldiers. Other Australian soldiers will keep the route.

The programme of welcome has indeed not been so much planned as evolved. It has grown with the demands of the people. Every hour yesterday saw additions and expansions until it has reached the dimensions of a national function. Commander Perrin and his assistants at the Royal Aero Club, who were responsible for the reception arrangements, had to put on a special staff to deal with inquiries and suggestions.

So far as the club is concerned, said Commander Perrin, yesterday, a deputation, headed by the committee, and composed of 200 members, will drive to the station in motor-cars. We propose bringing the Atlantic airmen to the club, where they will stay for a few minutes, but there will be no demonstration to-morrow night, as we do not intend to interfere with the real home-coming.

The reception committee will include the Duke of Atholl (chairman), Brigadier-General Sir Capel Holden, Major-General Sir W. S. Brancker, Major-General A. Ogilvie, Brigadier-General S. M. Maitland, Lieutenant-Colonel D. A. Grey, Lieutenant-Colonel J. D. Dunville, Lieutenant-Colonel T. O'Brien Hubbard, Lieutenant-Colonel Lloyd, Lieutenant-Colonel F. K. McLean, Mr. Handley Page, Mr. T. O. M. Sopwith, and Mr. G. B. Cockburn.

From the station to the club there will be a procession of motor-cars, each flying the sky-blue flag with the chocolate initials of the club. The road will be :—

EUSTON-ROAD,	LANGHAM-PLACE,
PARK-CRESCENT,	REGENT-STREET,
PORTLAND-PLACE,	NEW BURLINGTON-STREET.

The authorities at King's-cross Station are expecting a huge crowd and the platform will be barricaded, admission being for ticket-holders.

A representative body of employees from the Sopwith factory will be at King's Cross to-night to greet Mr. Hawker on his arrival. The employees have also arranged for a concert to take place to-night at the large factory at Ham, at which it is announced Mr. Hawker will be present, or at least will attend for a brief interval. The great reception, so far as the Sopwith factory is concerned, is being arranged for to-morrow at the factory, where Mr. Hawker is so well known.

On Friday the Royal Aero Club will entertain Mr. Hawker and Commander Grieve at a luncheon at the Savoy Hotel, and as the function will be limited to members they are required to apply to Commander Perrin for tickets.

It is hoped that arrangements will be completed in time for a great flying demonstration in Mr. Hawker's honour to be held at the London Aerodrome, at Hendon, on Saturday and Sunday afternoons next, May 31 and June 1. Mr. Hawker is to give looping and exhibition flights on a high speed Sopwith scout machine, and he will afterwards make some passenger flights.

MRS. HAWKER'S STEDFAST FAITH.

" I AM SURE HE WILL RETURN."

As evidence of Mrs. Hawker's absolute conviction that her husband would return, the following correspondence is interesting.

On May 21 Lord Northcliffe saw Mrs. Hawker with regard to the suspense which she was undergoing, when she expressed the firm conviction that there was no need for anxiety.

On the morning of the 23rd the announcement was published that the Daily Mail would divide the prize between the next-of-kin of the two airmen. Thereupon Mrs. Hawker wrote the following note to Lord Northcliffe :—

I enclose a letter to the Editor of the Daily Mail in regard to the proposal in this morning's paper that in the event of the airmen never returning the amount of the prize money should be given to their next-of-kin in proportion as previously arranged by them.

While appreciating this as a very noble offer, I cannot and will not, as you know, believe that my husband is not alive. I am sure that he will soon return to hear of the generosity of the *Daily Mail* and your personal kindness to me at this time.

The letter enclosed was as follows :—

To the Editor of the *Daily Mail.*

Sir,—With firm faith in the power of God to succour my husband and companion wherever they fell, but with a lonely heart, I thank you for your most generous offer, following the many kindnesses you and your staff have shown to me during this anxious week.

Whenever the time comes for my trouble to be relieved, among my happiest duties will be that of teaching our little Pamela that her father did not hesitate to venture all for the honour and glory of the country.—Yours truly,

May 23.   MURIEL HAWKER.

THE KING TO MRS. HAWKER.

MANY MESSAGES OF CONGRATULATION.

Mrs. Hawker has received the following telegram from the King :—

The King rejoices with you and the nation on the happy rescue of your gallant husband. He trusts that he may be long spared to you.—STAMFORDHAM.

Queen Alexandra telegraphed :—

With all my heart I wish you and the nation joy on the safety of your gallant husband and his companion. I rejoice that a Danish ship rescued his precious life.—ALEXANDRA.

The Secretary of the Air Council telegraphed yesterday morning to Mr. Hawker and Commander Grieve congratulating them upon their safety, and expressing admiration for their gallant attempt. Similar messages were sent to Mrs. Hawker and Captain Mackenzie-Grieve (father of Lieutenant-Commander Grieve).

Among the American messages received by the Air Ministry is the following telegram from Lieutenant-Colonel Glendinning, of the U.S. Air Service, Philadelphia :—

Warmest congratulations. Your kingdom should be proud of so brave and heroic a subject. Every American citizen rejoices with you upon his recovery, and praise in open admiration the valour of your countrymen.

The American Naval Headquarters in London sent congratulations to Mrs. Hawker, the British Admiralty, the Air Ministry, and the Royal Aero Club. To the Air Ministry the message was as follows :—

Admiral Benson, Chief of Operations of the U.S. Navy, and I wish to express our extreme gratification and relief for the welcome news of the rescue of Mr. Hawker and Commander Grieve.—(Signed) ADMIRAL KNAPP.

Among the many messages received by Mrs. Hawker was the following telegram from Lord Northcliffe :—

Please let me express my delight at the accuracy of your prediction of Wednesday last.—NORTHCLIFFE.

Mr. W. M. Hughes, Prime Minister of Australia, telegraphed to Mr. Hawker :—

Heartiest congratulations on your magnificent effort and your safe return. The one has filled all Australians with lasting pride and the other has lifted a burden from our hearts and minds which was becoming far too heavy. Advance, Australia!

COMMANDER GRIEVE.

NAVIGATOR'S PART IN THE FLIGHT.

Commander Mackenzie-Grieve, whose magnificent work as Mr. Hawker's navigator is not generally appreciated, is returning to his home at Droxford, in Hampshire, in two or three days, and the village, which is exceedingly proud of his exploit, is arranging to give him a hearty welcome. He is expected to stay in London in order to deliver to the King the message handed to him by the Governor of Newfoundland just before his departure.

Commander Mackenzie-Grieve, with his parents, has been resident at Fir Hill for many years. Droxford is also Admiral Sir Doveton Sturdee's village. Commander Mackenzie-Grieve's father is Captain Grieve, a retired naval officer, who was yesterday the recipient of many messages and telegrams of congratulation, and also of two telegrams from his son.

It is not the first time that Captain Grieve's household has had to bear anxiety about his son's safety, for he was on the Campania when she met with an accident in the Firth of Forth. Commander Grieve, who was at one time in H.M.S. Revenge, is 30 years of age and a bachelor.

Some indication may be given of the nature and responsibilities of the navigating officer in a Transatlantic flight. The report published on Saturday showed that the aeroplane was sighted by the cable ship Faraday at a point which is within a mile or two of the regular steamer track. It would appear, therefore, that Commander Mackenzie-Grieve had been able to keep his machine up to that point on the track he had laid down.

The difficulties to contend with in a flight across the Atlantic are (1) the question of the reliability of the engine and the petrol range of the machine ; and (2) the determination of position with sufficient accuracy that the navigator may be assured that he is keeping to his proper track. The first was the concern of the pilot, Mr. Hawker. With regard to the second, the difficulties of navigation, a course can be steered by compass within a degree or two, but unless the air navigator knows with accuracy the direction and force of the wind he will be unable to make suitable allowances for leeway.

Various methods have been proposed for the estimation of the wind, of which the most practicable consists of dropping a smoke bomb or flare into the sea and noting the exact direction in which it goes astern. There is, unfortunately, a difficulty in doing this with any certainty from a height of 8,000 or 10,000 feet, which is the economical height for petrol consumption. The navigator has therefore to depend principally for his position on observations of the sun or stars, or alternatively, on directional wireless.

In all these respects Mackenzie-Grieve was well equipped with instruments; he had long experience of the navigation of ships, and the fact that he was sighted where he was shows that he must have overcome the difficulties attendant on the adaptation of ship's navigation to aircraft.

The task of Commander Mackenzie-Grieve was very different from that of the American seaplanes which flew to the Azores. The N.C. 4 and its companions had merely to fly from one point to another fifty miles away, and, except for a short distance, they were hardly ever out of sight of one of their beacon lights. Mackenzie-Grieve, on the other hand, has shown that it is possible to navigate an aeroplane 1,100 miles over the sea through unknown winds and without speaking a single ship, and to be at the end of that time no more than a mile or two from the track he had prescribed for himself. Even by their failure they have made as great an advance in the navigation of the air as Columbus did in the navigation of the ocean.

He and Hawker have failed in their attempt, but they have succeeded in showing that the navigation of aeroplanes across the Atlantic does, in the hands of a trained and skilful navigator, present no insuperable difficulties. They have carried forward long-distance oversea aerial navigation to a point that brings us within sight of the time when aeroplanes can voyage " coastwise, cross-seas, round the world and back again."

WEDNESDAY, MAY 28, 1919.

MR. HAWKER IN LONDON.

A GREAT WELCOME TO THE AIRMEN.

MOBBED BY CHEERING CROWDS.

ROYAL RECEPTION TO-DAY.

The home-coming last evening of Mr. Hawker and Commander Grieve, the heroes of the daring attempt to fly across the Atlantic, was marked by scenes of extraordinary enthusiasm.

A series of popular demonstrations by cheering crowds at Scottish and English railway stations on the homeward route culminated in an unprecedented exhibition of mingled joy and pride at its close. Led by Australian soldiers, great crowds which had gathered at King's Cross Station and in the streets through which the airmen passed in procession to the Royal Aero Club gave them an uproarious welcome.

The King will receive Mr. Hawker and Commander Grieve at Buckingham Palace at 10.30 this morning, when they will give to his Majesty an account of their Atlantic adventure.

The airmen will afterwards be entertained by the *Daily Mail* at the Savoy Hotel, where the £5,000 awarded to them by that journal in recognition of their gallant effort will be presented to them.

LONDON'S FIRST GREETING.

AUSTRALIAN SOLDIERS AND THEIR HERO.

Mr. Hawker is an Australian, and Australia took his reception at King's Cross Station into her own hands. Other people were there, of course—a multitude of other people—but it was the Australian soldiers who predominated in the crowd, distinguished it from ordinary crowds, and contributed with gentle force to keeping it safe from harm. The force of organization they brought to bear was perhaps a trifle irregular and unconventional, but had a great deal to do with preventing any very serious accident to one of the biggest, most excited, and ardent, but one of the best-tempered throngs that has ever gathered in a London railway station.

More than once the broad shoulders of Australian soldiers were set against ugly rushes, and their quick hands upheld those who had slipped and ran the risk of being run over in the hurly-burly. They finished their conquest by taking bodily possession of Mr. Hawker and Commander Grieve, and delivering them to the acclamations of the populace outside in the road.

THE WAITING CROWD.

The train was timed for 7 o'clock. Soon after 5 o'clock men and women—and as many women as men—took what places they could get at the barrier of No. 1 arrival platform. About 5.30 wounded English soldiers and others began to arrive on the platform itself, and then the Australians marched in to rank themselves in the adjoining station roadway. They were headed by one who bore aloft the Australian flag, and by a young woman. Nothing had been definitely arranged by them. The assurance was given that their share in the reception was to be " quite informal " (as it proved), and that they were " just men who happened to be on leave."

Later on aviation old and new was well represented. Members of the Aero Club were there, with administrators and flying-men of reputation. These included Lord Montagu of Beaulieu, General Sir W. S. Brancker, General Holden, Colonel Dunville, Mr. T. Marlowe, Mr. Handley Page, Mr. R. Carey (of the Sopwith Company), Commander F. K. McLean (who flew up the Thames in days when that was a feat), Commander Perrin, Mr. Sydney Pickles,

Colonel Spencer Gray, D.S.O., Colonel Warwick Wright, D.S.O., Mr. Ralston, Mr. C. Fox, and Mr. J. E. Withers. Mr. W. O. Rancis represented the Aviation Section of the United States Army. A brilliant figure was Lieutenant Louis Noel, in light khaki uniform and gold lace, and with a line of decorations across his breast; he was present to show the fellow-feeling of French pilots. To this company descended from the station bridge, in long procession, the Mayor of St. Pancras and members of the Corporation in their robes, and headed by the mace-bearer.

The platform, for which permits were necessary, was pretty full by this time; and not only had the company at the barrier largely increased, but part of the bridge and the steps leading from it to the two neighbouring platforms accommodated a little host of sightseers. The peculiar Australian cry was ululating under the roof with odd echoes.

UPROARIOUS GREETING.

As soon as the engine-smoke of the train was seen there arose a tremendous shout of welcome, to which most other shouts of welcome seemed but faint whispers. The privileged people on the platform found themselves overwhelmed. Where a moment before was a quietly talking party was now a crushing, panting, laughing surge of all sorts and conditions. For reinforcements—unauthorized, it is to be feared—appeared from nowhere in particular, and the Australians, disdaining the road, joined in the medley.

Mr. Hawker and Commander Grieve were in the first carriage, and everybody wanted to be there at once. The Mayor was left in the background. Aldermen in their robes struggled to get ahead of tall soldiers. Ladies stood on tiptoe and cried, "There he is!" at every head which hung out of a carriage window.

During some moments it looked as though Mr. Hawker and his companion would never succeed in leaving their compartment. Australians leading the way, a hardy band of adventurers climbed to the roof of the train, till there appeared almost as many men up there as down among the striving mass of humanity on the level.

At intervals sounds were faintly heard which suggested that the band was playing—an Australian band drawn from the different depôts for the occasion. But what one really heard was a few thousand voices more or less melodiously engaged. Some sang "Australia will be there." Others sang "Auld Lang Syne," apparently under the impression that it was the nearest match to the other tune. A larger number merely shouted.

"CROWNED" AND LIFTED UP.

At last Mr. Hawker fell rather than stepped out of the train, and was received in friendly arms—whose it was impossible to decide. Both he and Commander Grieve looked pleased enough, but just a little scared, at their welcome. They were immediately "crowned" with two slouch Australian hats, which Captain Thompson, of the 30th Australian Battalion, had in readiness. This "crowning" is a ceremony by which Australia recognizes men as "Diggers," whether they be her own sons or

children by adoption. Commander Grieve was a son by adoption.

Very few could see all that was happening. Cries arose of "Lift them up," and accordingly they were lifted up, the cheers increasing, if possible, at the sight of them. For a few minutes there was a diversion in the shape of a rush from behind, and one was inclined to think that Corporation robes and khaki uniforms would never be disentangled.

CAR DRAWN BY SOLDIERS.

Somehow the two heroes were got to the cars which were waiting for them. Petrol, however, was regarded as too earthly a motive power for their deserts. As in other days the horses used to be taken out, so now the Australians, despising the engine, harnessed themselves with ropes to the car. With great difficulty the way was cleared, for the very road was compact with humanity.

Every Australian soldier who had been in the station tried to secure a place at the ropes. A few who failed made themselves reasonably content with looking on, but most triumphed in the effort to be worthy of dragging this most triumphant of cars. Nobody would have thought so many men could pull in so constricted a space. A halt was necessary, indeed, before the station gates could be reached. By some occult means Commander Grieve emerged from the strife and tumult on Australian shoulders, from which elevation he doubtless envied the comparative seclusion of Mr. Hawker, lost among a tangled knot of fiery spirits in the car.

Innumerable people, stretching densely as far as the eye could reach, were in waiting outside the station. Their hats could be seen in the air, and probably they were cheering. But no sound reached the gateway where the procession was looking for a chance of getting under way; so loud was the uproar there that no additional sound could edge in. The straining of ears to catch audible evidence that the outsiders were honestly making themselves heard only brought conviction that the ultimate had been reached in one's own neighbourhood, human faculty being, after all, limited, in this matter of hearing.

THE PROCESSION.

At last the procession did succeed in moving. It was rather a long one, motor-cars and trollies of various kinds going before and coming after the vehicle in which sat one of London's guests and the men who bore the other. They were bedecked with flags, British and Australian, and few failed to exhibit an inscription. "Both tails well up," said one. "Welcome home" was the motto of several more. In them, usually packed tightly, sat men and women waving small flags and adding their little to the babel of shouts and laughter.

Smiles always, and laughter at times, were as remarkable a side of the reception as its surpassing enthusiasm. Good temper reigned, the movement of the crowd, even at its thickest, being accompanied by the will to do the best in the circumstances. But for that, and the occasional efforts to which allusion has been made, the homecoming of Mr. Hawker and Commander Grieve might have been more uncomfortable. As it was, few wasted a thought on the drawbacks of an experience which in normal times would have struck them as rather terrifying. The common desire to honour the brave produced universal unselfishness.

UNRESTRAINED DELIGHT.

No man ever received a more rousing and affectionate welcome to London than Mr. Hawker and Commander Grieve did yesterday, nor one perhaps quite so palpably spontaneous and unrehearsed. There was more in it than the desire to acclaim a failure much more splendid than most successes; there was something of an almost selfish delight in that intense relief that comes from the cessation of pain. There is no revulsion like that which comes from a hope gradually and miserably given up and then on a sudden triumphantly realized.

All day long everybody had meant to be there, undeterred by the certain knowledge that everybody else meant to be there also. This resolution was hardened by the telegrams that poured in during the afternoon. Perth had risen with the dawn to greet the lost that were found; Edinburgh had carried them shoulder high; Newcastle had presented them with souvenirs. It was "up to" London to do something big, and London, like Todgers's, can do it if it pleases. "I think this beats the lot," said a little Cockney in the crowd who could not by any possibility see as much as "the 'oofs of the 'orses," though he added, with scrupulous generosity that the other cities had had to do it in their work time, and this was playtime.

A SURGING TIDE.

Walking up the Gray's-inn-road about six o'clock one could hear the murmur of the crowd before one could see it. Already a great tide of people was surging in front of King's Cross Station, and all the vantage points were occupied. It was a typical, motley, good-humoured London crowd. Many with little bags and umbrellas were clearly suburban "daily-breaders" who had missed their usual train to give Hawker a cheer. There were sailors and soldiers, especially Australian soldiers; decorous middle-aged ladies wearing gigantic fly-whisks of red, white, and blue paper, and screaming, giggling young ladies under the pleasing delusion that they occupied public attention; very small children on foot, and still smaller ones in perambulators. There were itinerant vendors of flags, picture postcards, and souvenir handkerchiefs—all doing a brisk trade. One very stout lady in a sealskin coat and large brass earrings had a tray full of "Models of 'Awker's aeroplane, all made to work," but these created a general and probably well-founded distrust. Not only were the pavements all crowded, but the parapet in front of St. Pancras Station was covered with opportunists sitting happy and straddle-legged over the heads of the mob.

Along the ever-narrowing streets omnibuses, vans, and cabs fought their laborious way. Every now and then came a motor-car with a light blue pennon bearing the initials of the Royal Aero Club. There were two or three be-flagged char-a-bancs from the Sopwith works, and several brakes of Australian soldiers, one of them with pipers at their head. A band of dirty, jolly little ragamuffin boys marched along, waving flags and beating old tins. The big clock over the station crept on with leaden hands, and the crowd grew thicker and thicker. The mounted police, in a friendly, almost deprecating, manner, pushed the people back, and the people, equally friendly, but perfectly determined, came back again to the old places as soon as the police had passed on. Boys and grown men also climbed into the trees and perched among the rickety perilous branches.

AERO CLUB TRIBUTE.

AIRMEN'S MODEST SPEECHES.

Mr. Hawker arrived at the Aero Club riding on a fine chestnut charger between two mounted policemen. He and his navigator received there a welcome as demonstrative as had been given them all along the route from King's Cross. Outside the gaily beflagged club premises in Clifford-street, a tremendous crowd had assembled, and in spite of the protection of his police escort it was only with the greatest difficulty that Mr. Hawker, hatless and showing signs of the treatment he had already received at the hands of his irrepressible admirers, was got into the club. The cheering which heralded his arrival had scarcely died down, when, five minutes later, Commander Grieve reached the club in a motor-car. This was the occasion for another outburst as hearty as that which had greeted Mr. Hawker.

Mr. Hawker, accompanied by his wife and mother-in-law and Mrs. Sopwith, was immediately escorted to the smoke-room, where he received the hearty congratulations of the large gathering of members who had assembled to greet him. Champagne was handed round and the company, lost no time in drinking to the health of the airman and his wife. No sooner had the glasses chinked than Commander Grieve, with his father and a host of followers, appeared, and his name was coupled with the toast and heartily drunk.

The 1919 Indianapolis 4.9 litre Sunbeam which Harry raced with great success at Brooklands.

Chapter Ten

Car Racing

Once Harry and his wife had returned from their well-deserved holiday he quickly got back to work to supervise the construction of the new floatplane Sopwiths were building as their entry in the first postwar Schneider Trophy race, to be held in 1919. The aeroplane was to be known as the Sopwith Schneider and was powered by a 450 hp Cosmos Jupiter engine.

The plane was finished by the end of August, so they took it down to Southampton to carry out trials and do the final preparations for the race which was to take place on 10 September 1919, at Bournemouth. Hawker sent his racing hydroplane, *Australia II*, down so he could go by sea between Southampton, where they were staying, and Hythe, where the aeroplane was housed.

Hawker was lucky to escape from what could have been a very serious accident on the maiden flight of this new plane which had special floats made to Hawker's design. After starting up the engine and opening up the throttle, the combined effect of the drag of the floats and the powerful thrust from the propeller, caused the front of the floats to immediately dig into the water and the tail came up until the aircraft was almost perpendicular.

As the cockpit was very small it was not the quickest thing to get out of in case of emergency. However it was only seconds before Hawker emerged, shouting to the mechanics on the slipway to hang on to the tail to prevent the machine sinking. They managed to beach the machine and it was discovered that, due to some miscalculation, the floats had been fitted too far back.

The machine was packed up in great haste as Hawker decided to take it back to Kingston that day. It was loaded on to a trailer, which for some reason had to be towed by Hawker's Sunbeam. The journey was done with some speed which was one advantage of the Sunbeam's big engine.

Two days later the repairs and alterations had been completed and the aeroplane returned to Hythe where very successful test flights were made during which it achieved a top speed of 180 mph.

There were four British entries for the Schneider Trophy Race so elimination trials were necessary as the rules restricted the entry from each country to three. These trials were to be held on 3 September at Cowes. However only three of the entries turned up. A Supermarine with a Napier Lion engine of 450 hp, piloted by Squadron Leader B.D. Hobbs, DSO, DFC; a Fairey also with a 450 hp Napier Lion, piloted by Lt Col V. Nicholl, DSO; and the Sopwith Schneider flown by Hawker.

Hawker had further problems on one landing when he struck a submerged object in the water, tearing the bottom off one of his floats. The aeroplane immediately started to sink. He succeeded in getting back to shore by manoeuvring a rowing boat under the damaged float. Replacement floats had to be secured quickly. The broken ones were removed and put in the boat to get them back to Hythe with the least delay possible.

Muriel's description of this journey tells the story:

"This hydroplane was designed to carry two people at speed, and not as a conveyance for a number of people and baggage, so it was with feelings of qualm that I took my seat beside Harry with my sister on my knees. The two floats were securely tied onto the bows, and with two men on the stern to balance we began heading toward the Solent. It did not take much movement to cause an alarming list, and Harry was continually calling out to 'Trim the boat!'

"Rounding the bend out of the harbour into the open sea the whole thing capsized, pitching everyone into the water. Only one of the party could not swim so he clung desperately to one of the floats.

"It is no joke to be suddenly dumped into the sea in heavy clothing as it gets so sodden that one has great difficulty in keeping one's head above water. Harry surfaced nearby and checked that the others had come to the surface. Fortunately our plight was noticed and a rowing boat put out from shore and picked us up, after what seemed an eternity but in reality was probably not long.

"A touch of comedy lightened the occasion when another boat put out with such haste that the would-be rescuers did not notice that the bung had not been put in place in the bottom of the boat so it was not long before it too foundered.

"A launch then arrived and we were able to get the hydroplane towed ashore. Harry immediately began to drain the water out of the engine, finding there was no serious damage, except that the magneto had suffered from the immersion. After dismantling and drying it out, he was able to continue the journey, this time without the floats.

"By now it was quite dark and, about half way across the Solent, the magneto failed again. Harry, who was by this time on his own, moored in the shelter, behind an anchored ship, where he was able to get the magneto going again and eventually arrived back at the hotel at 11 pm, still in wet clothes.

"My sister and myself and one other of the party, Mr Smith,

meanwhile had gone back to Southampton in a steam ferry. The captain, hearing of our trouble, allowed us to use the engine room to dry out during the one hour trip back.''

Replacement floats were sent down from Kingston and fitted, but the race turned out to be a fiasco. There were seven competitors in all, three French and one Italian, as well as the British. Although the day began with perfect weather, just at the time the race was due to start a thick fog descended, completely blotting out the turning points on the course.

Hawker had damaged a float again and saved the day by landing close to the beach so that the machine could be pulled onto the beach before it could sink.

The fog failed to lift and it was impossible to run the contest. The Italian did some circuits at a terrific speed but it was observed that he did not follow the correct course so he could not be awarded the Trophy. Ultimately it was decided that this 1919 race should be declared "no race". It was agreed that it should be held the following year in Italy.

After this race it had been arranged that Hawker and his wife would travel to Scotland for a visit to Tom Sopwith so they could join him on a stag shoot. Hawker was an exceptional shot, and the previous autumn had bagged two stags in one day. Unfortunately they were prevented from going because of a railway strike, which was a great disappointment.

During the winter of 1919-20 there was little to be done in the way of flying. With the cessation of the war, activity in the aeroplane factories had collapsed. A period of great readjustment followed, with all the people who had been engaged in production of war equipment being suddenly discharged whilst at the same time, thousands were being demobilized from the armed forces. Unemployment reached massive proportions.

Hawker, along with all the others, suddenly found himself with very little to do and immediately looked round for any opportunity, as he could not bear to be idle.

His luck held and he seized with great enthusiasm the opportunity to drive a new six cylinder Sunbeam racing car which the Sunbeam Company had built for the Indianapolis 500 race in the USA. He was to try it out at Brooklands on Whit Monday, 1920, a public holiday.

He went down to Wolverhampton to inspect the car and was amazed at the care with which racing cars were produced. "The Sunbeam people do the whole thing properly," he said. The car was brought down from Wolverhampton to Brooklands a few days before the race, in time to give it several trial runs before the meeting. These proved more than satisfactory.

The meeting itself was a record event and the scene, even for Brooklands, was a memorable one.

(Upper left) Hawker standing beside his Mercedes which was powered by a 350 hp Sunbeam aero engine.

(Lower left) Hawker's Austro Daimler after failing to negotiate a bend on Aerodrome Road at Brooklands.

(Upper) The 12 cylinder, 225 hp racing Sunbeam after the smash at Brooklands, when several yards of corrugated iron fencing were torn down.

Hawker inspecting the valve gear of the 320 hp ABC engine in the Sopwith Rainbow aeroplane. It is interesting to note that, for racing, the exhaust stubs were removed to reduce drag.

"From the bottom of Test Hill to the entrance to the course, the track was lined on both sides with cars, while the hill was crowded with people, breathlessly following the fortunes of their favourites as the burnished bonnets of the great cars glittered like shooting stars round the great track."

The press reports left no doubt that Hawker was the popular figure of the day. Whatever he did, it seemed that he was a great favourite of the crowd. His first race in the Sunbeam was the Short Lightning Handicap, which he won from scratch after overhauling his most formidable opponent, a Vauxhall, just as they were entering the finishing straight. His average speed for the race was 98.5 mph.

His second victory was in the next race, the Long Lightning Race which was no less exciting, which he won by a car's length. When he was overtaking one competitor on a very bumpy part of the track the car jumped out of gear and he accidentally put it back into second gear. Before moving it into top gear the tachometer showed (for that time) an extraordinary high 5,700 rpm. However no engine damage could be found when it was subsequently dismantled. His best lap for the day was at an average speed of 106.65 mph.

Hawker was pleased with this most successful day. His wife Muriel was not there and writes in her book:

"It was a great disappointment to me not to have seen his first attempt at motor racing, but Mary was then just a few days old. She was born on the anniversary of Harry's departure on the Atlantic flight and was named after the vessel which saved him. I was reluctantly compelled to stay at home and be content with watching them set out in the car in the morning, receiving my reward when, just after tea, they all returned home bubbling with excitement after their successful day."

Motor racing became Hawker's latest passion and he immediately got to work on his own 12 cylinder Sunbeam which he proceeded to strip completely of any superfluous items, lamps, mudguards, windscreens etc., and to carry out some engine tuning. He was rewarded when he reached a speed of 107 mph.

Unfortunately, during the course of the race, one of the front tyres began to shed its tread at high speed, causing a series of violent skids from which he recovered with difficulty. Undeterred, he then considered making a properly streamlined body for the car.

Meanwhile Sunbeam had produced a new model, a 450 hp car, which had just arrived for trials. After taking it for a run, he was so impressed with its superior performance that he took his own Sunbeam home, restored it to street condition, fitted new tyres, and commented that a car which could only do 110 mph was only fit for touring, so ending its brief racing career.

The date set for the midsummer race meeting at Brooklands was 26 June 1920 and the 350 hp Sunbeam was to make its public debut. It arrived towards the end of the week and Hawker decided to take it for a lap or two in the morning before the meeting began. He started off early in the morning for Brooklands, leaving Muriel to follow later. When she arrived at Brooklands, while waiting in a queue to get in, she heard a shout, "Hawker has crashed!" She goes on to relate:

"What one does on these occasions is often hard to remember, but I know I got out of the stationary car and walked on to the paddock, almost dazed, to find out what had happened. Arriving at the gate, the sight of Harry standing there was such a relief, that instead of hurrying to tell him of the great anxiety of the last few moments, I could say nothing. He was surprised to see me walking in, and asked where the car was saying, 'You don't generally walk to Brooklands.' "

Harry's subtle humour was lost on Muriel on this occasion!

A press account of the accident related how horrific it was and the good fortune that it did not have more serious consequences. Hawker, indeed, had a charmed life, having cheated death on so many occasions.

"Hawker had the car out for just an ordinary race meeting practice run. On the banking, under the Member's Bridge, the car was doing 125 mph, beautifully, with plenty of power and speed in hand, a black snouted, white bodied speed monster, hurtling round in the fresh morning air, well up the banking, when the front offside tyre burst.

"A swerve, a struggle with the wheel, utter disaster barely averted, and with the front axle chattering uncushioned on the concrete, the car plunged on under its own momentum down the railway straight. Try as he will, he cannot get the car to respond to the wheel and bear left. The drag of the blown tyre stubbornly holds it to the right of the track.

"Careering almost parallel with the fence, which runs alongside the straight for almost a quarter of a mile, the car at last digs its front end into the corrugated iron fence. Still doing over 80 miles an hour, it rips the fence apart for 11 or 12 yards, charges on obliquely down a four foot drop, and finishes up on all four wheels right side uppermost, a paling jammed immovably in one of the front wheels but otherwise undamaged. Mr Hawker, too, seemed but little shaken by his experience and far more interested in the glorious running of his mount before taking the toss than the accident itself."

By this time he was having a considerable amount of trouble with his back which probably was a result of the flying and car accidents in which he had been involved. However, he refused to do anything about it and would not give up his flying and car racing.

The following weekend saw him back in the air at the Royal Air Force Tournament at Hendon, where a huge crowd had gathered to see the finest exhibition of flying ever seen. Hawker, in a Swallow monoplane, took it through a series of stunts which, according to one press report, were quite different from anything previously demonstrated.

The Aerial Derby of 1920 was to be held at Hendon on 24 July, but Hawker, who did not have a machine which was really competitive, was asked to come over to Hendon in the Swallow, just to entertain the crowd with aerobatics while the competitors were away on the race. However, the day before the race he could not resist the temptation to take part in the contest and decided to take a sporting chance and enter the Sopwith Rainbow. The Rainbow was the landplane version of the plane built for the 1919 Schneider Trophy race.

It had been rebuilt by Hawker, who converted it to a landplane and replaced the 450 hp Cosmos Jupiter engine with an ABC (All British Company) Dragonfly engine of 320 hp. These engines were found to suffer from serious mechanical problems due to torsional vibration of the crankshaft.

Due to his popularity he was immediately favoured to win, even though there were at least three faster machines entered.

Departures were to be made at intervals and the winner was to be determined on the time taken to complete the set course. Hawker was number 13 to start in the field of 16. The course was over two laps, each of 100 miles. Hawker completed the first lap in 41 minutes 31 seconds, overtaking one of the faster machines, a Bristol Bullet. The fastest machine in the race, a Nieuport Goshawk, was forced to land at Brooklands with engine trouble. The only faster plane left to pass was the Semiquaver which eventually finished the 205 mile course in 1 hour 18 minutes.

Hawker's time was 1 hour 23 minutes but he was ruled out of the race because he flew straight over the aerodrome as he had done in previous years. He was not aware that the race rules had been changed which required pilots to make a circuit of some pylons before landing. He was therefore denied second place which his elapsed time would have given him.

Unfortunately, when landing, the Semiquaver overturned, but the pilot, Mr Courtney, was not injured.

The Rainbow was again rebuilt when the ABC engine was replaced with a Bristol Jupiter engine of 500 hp which gave the Rainbow a top speed of 175 mph. It carried the same registration, G-EASI, before and after the two rebuilds.

Hawker was very busy during the next month. In one week he was required in three different places, as far apart as Cowes, Brooklands and Martlesham Heath, in Suffolk. The only way he could do this was by air and this would surely be one of the earliest occasions in which an aeroplane was used in the normal course of civilian business.

The Air Ministry had offered a prize of 13,000 pounds for the design and production of an aeroplane having speed and reliability. Companies were invited to submit machines to compete. Sopwiths submitted their Antelope, fitted with a Wolseley Viper engine. The only other main contender was a Westland aircraft fitted with a Napier engine. They were obviously looking for an aeroplane that could fulfil a peacetime role and, at the same time, support the aviation industry during the depression following the war.

The Antelope that Hawker was to demonstrate had an enclosed cabin for two passengers, and was fitted with comfortable arm chairs, sliding windows and a sliding panel in the roof. The chairs could be raised and one could have the benefit of an open roof. The cabin was fitted with hot and cold air controls and a speaking tube connection to the pilot's cockpit.

The tests covered slow flying, speed and economy, together with take-off and landing trials. In the slow flying test the Antelope recorded the lowest speed of 43 mph and in the speed trials reached 110.35 mph, the second best performance.

The landing tests consisted of an approach over a row of balloons, tethered 50 feet from the ground by threads, and landing in as short a distance as possible. The Antelope was outstanding and landed in 188 yards, the next best being a Napier entry which took 235 yards.

In the economy trials the Antelope took second place and took off with a run of 23 yards, just shorter than the Napier. There was also a "hands off" test during which the Antelope flew for 5 minutes.

Another part of the trial was for reliability and consisted of two 3½ hour flights with a passenger, to be carried out at a minimum speed of 80 mph and above 3,000 feet.

The final result was very hard to decide as the two aeroplanes were so closely matched, but the Air Ministry awarded the prize to the Napier Company which received 10,000 pounds and for second place Sopwiths received 3,000 pounds.

Another motor race had been arranged at Brooklands for 2 August in which Hawker was to drive the 450 hp Sunbeam monster again. It had been repaired after the crash through the corrugated iron fence. His wife was very fearful about Hawker racing again and left the two children in Bournemouth, where they were staying, and took the train to London and then drove the AC car to Brooklands.

The big Sunbeam was the scratch car and, after all the others had gone off, the engine stalled at the start and the car did not compete. Muriel was most relieved about this as she appeared to have some premonition of disaster. Perhaps fate took a hand here?

At this time Hawker had been staying at Martlesham and flying down almost every day to Cowes to help in the preparation of a powerboat being built by Saunders for the British International Trophy, at which he was going to drive. It was named the *Maple Leaf*

V, it was 39 feet long and powered by four, 12 cylinder Sunbeam engines of 400 hp each, giving a total of 1,600 hp.

Another boat *Maple Leaf VI*, to be driven by Lt Col A.W. Tate, DSO, was of similar hull construction but was powered by two Rolls-Royce engines together supplying 1,100 hp.

There were six British entries and elimination trials were run. Of the surviving four, *Maple Leaf V* was the leader, although the times were very disappointing, with an average of just over 30 knots.

Three American entries were sent over, *Miss Detroit*, *Miss America* (both powered by 800 hp Smith Marine Twin engines which were built up from twin Liberty V-type aero engines of 400 hp each), and a third boat *Whip-o'-will*, which burst into flames and sank.

The course was over a total of 33 nautical miles. Five rounds were to be raced and a time limit set to complete each round.

The first of these was run on 10 August when some desperate manoeuvring took place in an attempt to be first over the starting line. Hawker managed to get away first and the rest crossed shortly after. The boats soon settled down to an order which was maintained through the series. *Miss America, Miss Detroit, Maple Leaf V, Maple Leaf VI* and the French entry, *Despujols*, which was fitted with a Richard Brazier engine.

Hawker had engine trouble on the second round but was able to finish within the time limit on one engine. The five boats were, on average, within 4 minutes of each other on every round of the series. The average speed of *Miss America* was 53.42 mph.

The American boats were conspicuous by the manner in which they skimmed over the water, with very little apparent displacement and very little spray. It is interesting to note that the times were so close, considering the great variation in engine power. The British boats were obviously displacing a lot more water because of their heavier engines and the description of their runs confirms this. *Maple Leaf VI* could be distinguished in the distance by periodic banks of spray thrown up as she hopped along, and *Maple Leaf V* seemed to charge along between two walls of water. America won the Trophy for the fifth time since 1903.

Hawker was at Brooklands for further motor racing fixtures during September in which he was not very successful. In one race the AC car he entered was found by the scrutineers not to be standard and he was disqualified from entering. The next race he entered a perfectly standard four cylinder DFP car but he was so handicapped that he only reached the finishing straight as the cars for the next race were lining up.

The next event on the calendar was the Gordon Bennett Air Race of 1920 to be held at Etamps, France on 28 September.

Hawker's machine, the Rainbow had to be withdrawn a few days before the race due to Sopwiths' financial troubles. The other two

The classic Sopwith Schneider floatplane with a 450 hp Cosmos Jupiter engine built for the 1919 Schneider Trophy Race.

The Rainbow, this time with a 450 hp ABC engine. This aircraft was a rebuild of the Sopwith Schneider. It bears the same registration letters.

British entries were Raynham in the Martinsyde Semiquaver, which had won the Aerial Derby, and Tait Cox in a Nieuport Goshawk, which had also flown in the Aerial Derby. As the Nieuport Company had closed down some doubt was thrown on the eligibility of the Goshawk, but in any event it did not arrive in sufficient time to qualify for entry.

This left only one entry from Britain, and there were three each for America and France. The French had won the previous two races and if they could win this one they would win the Cup outright. The race was a time trial. Flying could begin any time after 7.00 am and the result was decided on the fastest time. It was not Britain's day, as Raynham had to abandon the race due to falling oil pressure.

Early in December it was arranged that Hawker should attempt to beat the world motor speed record for short distances with the 450 hp Sunbeam. Heavy rain during the morning prevented this. The track had dried, but not properly, by the afternoon but he took the car for a few laps anyhow. It was not a fair test due to the wet and greasy state of the track on which the tyres were unable to transmit all the power that was available. A speed of 125 mph was reached but the tachometer displayed revolutions equivalent to 140 mph, which indicated considerable wheel slip. This was a great disappointment and the attempt turned out to be a casualty of the English December weather.

Hawker at the wheel of the AC racing car. He designed the streamlined body which gave a greatly improved performance.

Chapter Eleven

A New Company

When World War I came to an end, Sopwiths' war contracts were immediately cancelled by the Government, including a large order for Snipes. This left Sopwiths in serious financial difficulty as they had a large amount of capital equipment and materials on hand for which there was no further use, plus a labour force of around 2,000 who had to be laid off immediately. They also had substantial taxation commitments, but struggled on until 1920 when they went into voluntary liquidation, paying all their creditors.

The reasons that led to the decision to wind up the company were set out in the September 1920 *Flight* magazine.

"The closing down of Sopwiths at Kingston conveys a lesson for all. In these works were constructed, during the war, some of the finest fighting aircraft possessed by any of the belligerent powers. When the Armistice came, putting an end to hostilities, the Directors, with their accustomed foresight, decided to employ the works in the manufacture of motor cycles, for which the plant was eminently adapted. They secured a magnificent design in the ABC and orders poured in for the new machines.

"In the interval, like many other firms, they have had to pay out wages before going into production and their resources have become exhausted. In the circumstances there appeared to be no alternative but to close down at once. We are quite satisfied that the management has done all it can to get into the production stage and, that the efforts which have been made have not been successful, is not to be laid at their door. But the payment of high wages for a low standard of production cannot be maintained for ever, and one day the inevitable is bound to happen.

"According to an official of Sopwiths, the ultimate decision was taken as a result of a slump in the motor trade. Valuable orders from all parts of the overseas Dominions and Scandinavia have been cancelled, and this state of affairs coupled with the competition from America, has made it impossible for a lucrative trade to be carried on. So far as we are competent to judge, there is a very wide market for motor vehicles if manufacturers can deliver the goods. It is too much, however, to expect people who have ordered a year or more ago to wait indefinitely for the completion of their orders, and quite naturally they turn elsewhere for their requirements.

"We trust most sincerely that some way out of an apparent impasse may yet be found and that the firm of Sopwith, with all its traditions in the field of aviation, will not disappear."

Sopwiths were not alone with these kinds of problems. The only firms that survived were the older established ones who had been involved in general engineering before the outbreak of war.

A group led by Hawker formed H.G. Hawker Engineering Company which was registered on 5 November 1920 with a capital of 20,000 pounds. The directors of the new company, drawn from the old Sopwith company, were H.G. Hawker, F. Sigrist, V.W. Eyre and the Company Secretary, F.I. Bennett. Tom Sopwith later joined the Board and, after Hawker's death, replaced him as Chairman.

Tom Sopwith was to lead Hawker Engineering through its most successful years. During this time many other aviation companies were taken over by Hawker Engineering. There was also a considerable amount of diversification into general engineering and other fields.

The Hawker Engineering company was to take over all the patent rights held by Sopwiths which covered aircraft, motorcars, motorcycles, internal combustion and steam engines. It also took over various contracts for the supply of spares and reconditioning the Snipes which had been adopted as the standard fighter in the newly formed Royal Air Force and remained in service until 1926. They were desperately looking for other products to make and turned their hand to anything they could produce to get established, even to manufacturing saucepans. One story goes that Hawker arrived in his office one morning to find a saucepan on his desk. When Sigrist came in Hawker said, "Well, Fred, what do you think of it? Saucepans! Where do I come in? I never thought I would live to find myself in a job that Mrs Beeton could do better than I." Mrs Beeton was famous for her cookbook.

Hawker Engineering had a momentous struggle to establish itself. Their first project, no doubt because of Hawker's previous experience and inclinations, was to build motorcycles. One of their most successful ventures was the construction of aluminium bodies for racing and sports cars. This of course flowed from Hawker's involvement with motor racing in the post-war period. In 1933 the name was changed to Hawker Aircraft Ltd. and shortly after it became the Hawker Siddeley Aircraft Company through the acquisition of Armstrong Siddeley Company. Although the Hawker Siddeley name remains, the aviation section of the Company was absorbed by British Aerospace Corporation in 1977.

Next, Hawker acquired a new AC car. This gained its name from Autocarriers Car Company Ltd which was set up in Surrey at

Sopwith and Hawker with one of the two-stroke motorcycles which were built by the Hawker Engineering Company.

Transatlantic Aviators' Dinner. From the left: Sir John Alcock, Sir Arthur Whitten Brown, H.G. Hawker, then Capt Fenn (in uniform), Lt Cdr Mackenzie Grieve, and on the right nearest the camera, F.P. Raynham and next to him Capt Morgan.

Thames Ditton in 1911. He had gone for a run in their latest model and was so impressed that he asked to see the drawings of the overhead valve engine. He saw possibilities for this as a racing car and bought it on the spot in chassis form. He experienced a lot of teething troubles with the engine but gradually worked up its performance. He then set about developing and equipping the car with a streamlined aluminium body. It was so successful that people began to suspect it was supercharged.

This body created a lot of interest and the factory started manufacturing car bodies. The AC's career was plagued with connecting rod and piston failure, dropping valve heads, and other mechanical troubles. On one occasion, whilst racing, a connecting rod smashed a great hole through the cast aluminium oil sump. Hawker then walked back along the track and picked up the offending connecting rod, which was still hot.

Unfortunately AC Cars could not supply a replacement sump so he was forced to patch it up. The magneto drive shaft had also been smashed and Hawker had to use his vast ingenuity to fabricate a

housing and magneto drive so that he could get the car on the track again. His wife tells of one incident when he was at high speed on the Byfleet banking on the Brooklands track:

"...After a lap or two at speed, unmistakable sounds proclaimed that the umpteenth valve head had broken. As it was only the day before it was to race at a meeting, this was a very serious matter, but Harry, nothing daunted, began to tie the tow rope on to the Minerva, saying, 'We'll be there when the starter's flag falls.' The Minerva was my car which Harry had fitted with an enclosed body and upholstered in Bedford cord for comfortable winter motoring. However, it soon degenerated into a travelling workshop for the AC, complete with tow rope and spares. I nearly always, less proudly, preceded the AC home, connected by a rope."

Eventually Hawker got the whole thing sorted out and the AC made its first public appearance at the Brooklands Easter meeting, where it created a great deal of interest. It had a terrific turn of speed for a one and a half litre engine. Unfortunately the race handicappers had seen something of its capabilities, with the result that it was so heavily handicapped that, in spite of its speed, it was only able to come second in two races, making spectacular runs right through the field.

Winning the 1,500 cc Scratch race at the Junior Car Club meeting, and a very interesting short sprint of 250 yards against another well-known car, Capt Fraser Nash's GN (Godrey & Nash), spurred Hawker on to enter more races and set new records. He was very anxious for the AC to be the first 1,500 cc car to reach 100 mph, which it did on 3 June. He also established world light car records by achieving 105.55 mph for the flying mile, and 61.43 mph for the standing mile. Those records caused a great sensation in the motor world and even the press showed some enthusiasm for his latest achievements.

He received many letters of congratulation from people interested in the first 100 mph light car. The true sporting atmosphere of Brooklands was conveyed in a genial letter of congratulation from Mr Lionel Martin, who was not too proud to say he had coveted the distinction for the Aston-Martin car. Harry's wife writes in her book that he appreciated this very much, as well as the hearty good wishes of Captain Nash who now realised that his car had met its match in the AC.

When practising for the Midsummer Meeting at Brooklands on 25 June Hawker had another very narrow escape from disaster. As he was about to enter the straight, doing about 100 mph, he suddenly appeared to slide down the banking and a huge cloud of dust enveloped him. One bystander remarked: "Hawker's off the track! He'll need his luck now!"

When they arrived at the scene he was standing by the track waving that he was all right. This was belied by his appearance which was terrible for his whole face was covered in blood, which he was wiping with a handkerchief. All he was interested in was finding help to remove the car from where it had ended up in the long grass as it had skidded right off the track.

The accident had been caused by the strap breaking which held down the bonnet, which flew back, cut him across the forehead and dazed him for a minute. It also smashed his brand new Triplex goggles. Later, holding his goggles up, splintered and covered in blood, he said, "Hang it all, these are my favourite goggles! Just fitted me before, only fit for the Triplex display window now!" (Triplex was a trade name for an unbreakable glass!)

The AC was towed home once again. Considering the bump it must have received going off the track at such speed, it suffered very little — the two front wheels were buckled and were replaced with two new ones. The whole of that night was spent taking the body off to see if there had been any structural damage. Hawker raced the car again the next day at Brooklands but engine trouble prevented him from winning any races.

At some of these meetings both Hawker and Sopwith entered motorcycle races on machines they had produced.

No doubt with a view to the future, Hawker established an agency in Australia for DFP cars, being the initial letters of the Doriot, Flandin et Parrent Company which built them in France. As things turned out, he did not have the chance to exploit this agency.

The Nieuport Goshawk aeroplane, G-EASK, in which Hawker met his tragic death. Once again the exhaust stubs have been removed for racing.

Chapter Twelve

Final Flight

Harry Hawker had agreed to pilot a Nieuport Goshawk biplane in the Aerial Derby on 6 July 1921. Although the Nieuport was a French design it was built in England by the Nieuport & General Aircraft Co Ltd, which was formed in 1914 with a factory at Cricklewood. It thus qualified to race as a British machine.

Another pilot had already reached a speed of 166 mph in this machine. As this was a very prestigious race it was vital that the British machine should beat the French aces, who had reported higher speeds. Hawker's reputation was such that it was felt that he would have the best opportunity of getting the most out of the Goshawk.

On Saturday 9 July a telegram arrived at his home.

"Hawker, Ennadale, Hook Road, Surbiton. Machine ready for flying Tuesday afternoon.

Folland"

The test flight was arranged for the following Tuesday, 12 July.

Hawker rode to Hendon from his home at Hook on his motorbike. Arriving at about 5 pm, he carried out preparations for the test flight, and took off about half an hour later. The take-off was normal and the aeroplane climbed to about 2,500 feet. After a short time it was seen to make a sharp turn to the left and descend in a steep dive, during which flames appeared round the fuselage. It appeared to pull out of the dive but was then too low to avoid violent contact with the ground and was completely wrecked, throwing Hawker out with injuries so bad that, according to eyewitness reports, he died some 10 minutes later.

The Coroner's report stated that:

"Hawker died of injuries caused by the smashing to the ground of the aeroplane in which he was flying. and of which he had lost control owing to his physical disability."

The doctor's postmortem report stated:

"The mass of blood on the front of the spinal cord indicated that the haemorrhage was the cause of the accident."

The fact that Hawker had ridden his motorbike from Hook that morning and showed no discomfort, casts serious doubts on the

(Upper) Some of the remains of the Nieuport Goshawk
after the fatal crash.

(Lower) Floral tributes being taken to Hawker's grave, at Hook in Surrey, on the 225 hp Sunbeam. The driver is his brother-in-law, Capt L Peaty.

opinion of the doctor who conducted the postmortem, and his findings that this had been the cause of the accident.

There had been considerable disagreement as to whether the machine had been on fire in the air as many eyewitnesses stated they had seen flames. This was not to be finally resolved until the release of the official report by the Accident Investigation Branch of the Air Ministry which, for reasons unknown, had been marked "Secret" and stamped "Not to be released for 50 years". It was therefore not available to the Coroner, and it was not until the release of the document in 1972 that the real facts became known.

Eyewitness accounts agree that he lived for about 10 minutes after the crash so the haemorrhage could have occurred after the impact. This must have been the case for the official report clearly states that fire did occur well before the aircraft struck the ground and was the cause of the accident.

The accident report is reproduced in full on the following pages.

Bearing in mind Hawker's practical nature, and his almost complete disregard for keeping records of any kind, his failure to renew his pilot's licence mentioned in clause 3(d) of the report does not appear to be of any significance. He could quite easily have overlooked the fact that it was due for renewal.

The tragic conclusion to the test flight can only be described as the greatest single blow to his family, his country and the aviation industry that it could be possible to imagine. The only consoling factor is that his recurring back trouble was the symptom of deep seated and extensive tubercular disease, the seriousness of which only became apparent during the postmortem examination and which would have in any case given him a limited expectation of life.

To have a full understanding of clause 3(m) of the report, the following details of the engine will clarify the matter. It was an ABC, the largest static radial engine in production. It had 9 cylinders with a collector ring or manifold at the back of the engine. In order to keep the three carburettors cool they were mounted in front of the engine with induction pipes passing back between the cylinders. The defect in design which did not provide for locking the carburettor tops to prevent them coming unscrewed was nothing short of criminal considering there was, at that time, extensive knowledge of building aircraft and engines and the need for fastening everything.

One is left to conjecture how far Harry Hawker would have risen in the aircraft industry had the accident not claimed his life at the early age of 32.

The following tributes give some idea of the high regard in which he was held:

"The nation has lost one of its most distinguished airmen, who by his skill and daring has contributed so much to the success of British aviation."

H.M. King George V

"The nation is poorer for the loss of one who always displayed such splendid courage and determination. To such pioneers we owed our supremacy of the air during the war."

Rt Hon D. Lloyd George

The funeral cortege of Harry George Hawker, MBE, AFC.

CIVIL ACCIDENT C-43.

NIEUPORT "GOSHAWK" G-E.A.S.K.

Nr. HENDON 12.7.21.

AIR MINISTRY

C.G.C.A.

ACCIDENTS INVESTIGATION BRANCH.

Accident to Nieuport "Goshawk"   Engine 360 H.P. "Dragonfly"
        G-E.A.S.K.   No. 1.A.III.

OWNERS: Messrs. Nieuport and General Aircraft Company Ltd.

PILOT: Mr. H.G. Hawker, M.B.E., A.F.C.   (Killed)

Test Flight from Hendon Aerodrome, 12th July, 1921.

1. REPORT.

By telegram received at 1000 hours on 13.7.21.
The scene of the accident was visited the same
morning.

2. BRIEF DESCRIPTION.

At about 1730 hours the pilot arrived at Hendon and
the aeroplane was taken from the shed for the first
test of machine and engine since overhaul.   About
half an hour later the pilot took off and climbed
steeply to about 2,500 feet in a gradual turn to
the left.   When about 1 mile West of the aerodrome
the machine was seen to turn sharply to the left and
then descend in a steep dive, during which a
flame appeared round the fuselage.   At a low
height the aeroplane assumed a normal glide, in
which attitude it struck the ground at high speed
and was completely wrecked, at the same instant
bursting into flames.   The pilot, whose body was
thrown about 50 yards from the wreckage, was killed.

3. FACTS ESTABLISHED.

From consideration of the evidence the following facts
are regarded as established:-

(a) The aeroplane (the only one of its type) was built
     at the Nieuport Works, Hendon and first flown on
     17th June, 1920 for a speed record at Martlesham
     Heath.   It competed in last year's Aerial Derby
     but was forced to land at Brooklands owing to an
     engine defect.   In the following September the
     machine was flown to France for the Gordon Bennett
     race but did not arrive in time to take part and

was returned to England by air at the end of
October, 1920. From that date it was stored at
Hendon until recently overhauled and prepared
for this year's Aerial Derby.
The engine was completely overhauled about a
month ago at Messrs White's of Cowes and re-
installation was just completed before the flight
in question. The total flying time of the
aeroplane and engine was about 6 hours.

(b)   Three carburetters were employed on this engine
and these were situated in front of the cylinders,
with jacketted branch pipes leading to a common
induction manifold at the back. The carburetters
were inside the cowling and pipes were provided
for draining off petrol flooding from the jets.
The heating jackets were not in use. The open
exhaust ports were in close proximity to and behind
the carburetters.

(c)   The mechanic of the Nieuport Company, who assembled
the carburetters, and the representative of the
A.B.C. Company, who finally passed the engine, state
that all float chamber covers were screwed up tight
before the flight commenced.

(d)   The pilot was exceptionally experienced, particularly
on scout types of aeroplane, but he appears to have
done very little flying this year and had not
previously flown this particular machine.
For more than 12 months the pilot had suffered
from tuberculous disease of the spine, causing
great pain and restricted movement in his back,
and he had been strongly urged to undergo treatment
at the hands of a specialist.
He was granted a Pilot's Licence No.109, Class B,
on 30th May 1919, which was renewed on dates 30.11.19,
30.5.20 and 31.12.20; the tuberculous disease of
the spine being noted on the last occasion. This
licence expired 12 days before the accident and
had not been renewed.

(e)   The weather conditions for flying were good.
Bright sunshine, with a very light Northerly wind.

(f)   As the aeroplane left the ground the engine cut out
but picked up again immediately and after spluttering
a little, appeared to run satisfactorily.
The machine climbed steeply turning to the left in
a wide circle and when about one mile West of the
aerodrome, at a height of about 2,500 feet, the
tail was seen to move sharply to left and right
several times, after which the machine made a
banked turn to the left and then went into a steep
dive with the engine on. A few seconds later a
large flame appeared, for an appreciable length of
time, under the fuselage from the front of the
engine, and then went out and no further evidence
of fire was seen during the dive. A gradual
recovery from the dive was made and at a height of

about 50 feet the aeroplane assumed a normal glide, turning to the left, and finally flying into the ground at high speed.   The machine was enveloped in flames immediately on impact with the ground and before coming to rest.   It was completely destroyed by fire.

(g)   The engine had not been run in the machine since overhaul.   The pilot tested it on the ground and expressed himself as satisfied, although slight missing occurred on one magneto and the engine did not give more than 1,440 r.p.m. on both magnetos. The tanks contained 24 gallons of petrol.

(h)   The pilot came to Hendon from Kingston on a motor bicycle and shortly after arrival got into the aeroplane.
There is reason to believe that the safety-belt was not fastened before he left the ground.

(i)   The pilot breathed for about 10 minutes after the accident.   He was found lying about 40 yards beyond the burning wreckage and about 12 yards to the left of the track of the machine.   His feet and ankles were bare.   The grass in the vicinity of the body was smouldering.
The shoes were picked up about 20 yards from the spot where the aeroplane first struck the ground and approximately 90 yards from the body.
According to the evidence of several witnesses the pilot was standing in the machine when it first struck the ground.

On examining the wreckage it was found that:-

(j)   With the exception of the steel fittings and a few charred fragments of timber, the machine had been completely destroyed by fire and parts of the engine fused.

(k)   The aeroplane had landed in a large field and first touched the ground, with the undercarriage wheels, 48 yards from the hedge on the South side.   The marks of the wheels terminated at a deep hole in the ground, about 8 feet long, made by the machine which had then bounced twice for distances of 40 and 26 yards.   The front petrol tank was thrown 72 yards beyond the main wreckage and the two other fuselage tanks about 12 yards on each side.   An area of grass approximately 140 x 20 yards was burnt.

(1)   The principal bracing wires of the aeroplane could be traced and these were found to be intact.
All control cables were intact, except the aileron balance wire which bore evidence of having been broken in the crash.

-4-

(m) The float chamber cover of the bottom carburetter was
completely unscrewed (4 threads) but was prevented
from falling off by a throttle control rod. (These
covers screw down on to a fibre washer and are not
provided with any locking device). The float, as a
result of impact, was jammed at an angle in the chamber.
The condition of this float chamber cover was observed
before the engine was sufficiently cool to be touched.

(n) No other defects could be found in the engine other
than those due to impact or fire.

On examining the pilot's body and clothing it was found
that:-

(o) The neck, right ankle and left forearm were fractured,
and burns on the body were distributed as follows:-
Both ankles, from the top of the shoes upwards for
about 6 inches; right knee and outside of right leg;
back of right hand and forearm; a small patch on the
left knee. The hair on the right side of the head
was slightly singed.
The burns, which did not extend below the top layer
of skin, were all of a similar nature and had been
caused by liquid petrol burning on the skin. The
right ankle appeared to have been fractured after
burning.

(p) Except in the vicinity of the body burns, the pilot's
clothing was undamaged by fire.

(q) The shoes, of brown leather, were completely blackened
and charred on the surface of the uppers, soles and
heels. The leather of the insteps, however, was
practically undamaged by fire where protected by the
rudder-bar and bore impressions of aluminium.

By a Post Mortem examination it was found that:-

(r) Extensive tuberculous disease of the spine existed
and a large abscess, adjacent to the affected part,
had burst.

(s) The diseased condition of this part of the body was
such as to lead to paralysis of the legs within a
very short time and only additional pressure, by a
further formation of pus or by hemorrhage, was
required to produce that effect.
Hemorrhage had taken place before death.

(t) The extent to which the pilot's legs would have been
affected by the pressure on the spinal cord cannot be
estimated but the loss of power would have been
greater in the left leg than in the right and
confined to the lower limbs. The physical pain
caused by hemorrhage would be extremely severe.

-5-

4. SUMMARY OF FACTS RELATIVE TO FIRE IN THE AIR.

(a.) The cover of the bottom carburetter had come unscrewed in the air.

(b) Flames were seen coming from the front of the engine and would coincide with the ignition and burning out of the petrol in the bottom carburetter after the petrol had been cut off.

(c) The pilot's shoes were charred with the exception of the portion of the instep protected by the rudder bar.

(d) The pilot's ankles were burnt, but the portion of the feet corresponding to the shoes were unburnt. The shoes were found 90 yards from the body. The burns were therefore sustained in the air and not on the ground.

5. OPINION.

(a) That the accident was due to fire in the air caused by the escape of petrol through the unscrewed cover of the bottom carburetter and subsequent ignition by the exhaust gases.

(b) That the pilot succeeded in subduing or putting out the flames but was unable to properly control the aeroplane when landing owing to physical disability caused by burns and spinal hemorrhage.

G.B. COCKBURN.

for Controller General of Civil Aviation.
(Accidents Investigation Branch).

Air Ministry,
Kingsway, W.C.2.
11 August, 1921.

*Civil accident C-4-3
Nieuport 'Goshawk' G-E A'
Near Hendon 12-7-21*

Chapter Thirteen

Amalgamation

The period after Hawker's death was well documented in a paper read to the Institution of Mechanical Engineers at the Kingston College of Technology, Kingston on Thames, on 28 November 1968 by John Crampton DFC, AFC and Bar, MRAeS. In it he traced the development of the Hawker Engineering Company after the death of Harry Hawker. John Crampton was, at that time, Technical Sales Manager (Harrier) for Hawker Siddeley Aviation, later British Aerospace, until his recent retirement. He has most graciously given the author permission to use this paper as a basis for much of the following history.

Hawker Engineering was, at the time of Hawker's death, on firm ground with plenty of work in hand. Most of the old Sopwith factory was occupied and, while general engineering and motorcycle work diminished, more and more Sopwith Snipes were returned to the works for reconditioning. In the following year, Capt B. Thomson was appointed Chief Designer. He submitted two designs in answer to Air Ministry specifications, both of which were accepted. The first was for a two-seater reconnaissance monoplane, the Hawker Duiker. The second was a single-seater night fighter, the Hawker Woodcock. The Duiker was not a success but the Woodcock eventually saw squadron service in the RAF.

By the beginning of 1924 Capt Thomson had been replaced as Chief Designer by Mr W.G. Carter who, in 1916, had been the Senior Design Draftsman of Sopwiths. Carter redesigned the Woodcock and by so doing earned the company its first production contract.

A year earlier, in 1923, a young draftsman who had been with Martinsyde since 1914, joined Hawker Engineering. His name was Sydney Camm. He worked with Carter on the redesign of the Woodcock and displayed such exceptional talent that he was put in charge of the Cygnet Project. The result was a great success. Two Cygnets were built and won high praise at the Air Ministry Light Aeroplane Competition at Lympne in 1924. In the following year a Cygnet won the 100 mile International Handicap Race. The pilot was Flt Lt George Bulman, who subsequently became the company's chief test pilot and who remained with Hawker Engineering until 1945.

Carter left the company in 1925. Sydney Camm (later Sir Sydney Camm) took his place and held the position of Chief Designer for 34 years until 1959 when he was made Chief Engineer.

The first of Camm's military designs was the Danecock, a further development of the Woodcock, destined for Denmark. Three of these aircraft were built at Kingston on Thames in 1925 and were delivered in February 1926. Powered by the Armstrong Siddeley Jaguar engine, the Danecock was the first designed and built aeroplane to be exported by Hawker Engineering. It was the forerunner of hundreds that were ordered to equip air forces throughout the world, and contributed to the value and prestige of Britain's aircraft industry. Danecocks were subsequently built under licence in Denmark, remaining in service there until 1937. One such machine is preserved today in the Copenhagen Science Museum.

Apart from the Hurricane, the best known of all the aircraft produced by Hawker Engineering were the Hart and Fury biplanes. In June 1928 the prototype Hart first flew at Brooklands in the hands of Flt Lt George Bulman. The Hart first saw service in 1930 with No. 33 Squadron at Eastchurch. The Fury went into production in 1931 and No. 43 Squadron RAF at Tangmere was the first to be equipped with this outstanding single-seater interceptor fighter. One variation, the Demon, was supplied to the Royal Australian Air Force.

By 1933 any pretence at general engineering had disappeared so the name was changed to Hawker Aircraft Limited. In the following year Hawker Aircraft bought the Gloster Aircraft Company.

In July 1935 Tom Sopwith announced the formation of a Trust to acquire all the shares of Armstrong Siddeley Development Company, founded in 1919 by Mr J.D. Siddeley (who later became Lord Kenilworth).

This new powerful group of companies, known as the Hawker Siddeley Aircraft Company, included Armstrong Whitworth Aircraft Limited, Armstrong Siddeley Motors Limited, Air Service Training Limited and A.V. Roe and Company Limited plus the Hawker and Gloster Companies. In 1936 Hawker Aircraft Limited bought Parlaunt Park Farm at Langley, near Slough in Buckinghamshire, where a factory and airfield were constructed.

By 1936 Hawker Siddeley had a capital of six million pounds and so were ready and able to face the nation's call at the time of the Munich crisis. This financial security enabled this comparatively small company to go ahead with the development of Camm's next great project.

In 1933, with the Fury biplane well established in the RAF and production contracts in hand for foreign governments, Camm directed his thoughts toward the development of a monoplane fighter. Initially this machine took the form of a redesign of the Fury with a low cantilever wing and a steam-cooled Rolls-Royce Goshawk engine. By January 1934 it was clear that better performance could be obtained from the Rolls-Royce V12 liquid-cooled engine. Detailed design on what became known as the "Interceptor Monoplane" began in May 1934. In September that year a new design was submitted for evaluation to the Air Ministry.

On 21 February 1935 Hawker Siddeley received a contract to build one high speed monoplane, based on a design submitted on 4 September 1934, known as the F 36/34 single-seat fighter. Construction began at once. In September 1935 the new Rolls-Royce engine, now officially named the Merlin, was installed in the airframe and Flt Lt Bulman carried out the first flight on 6 November from Brooklands in the prototype of an aircraft that became known as the Hurricane. By March 1936 the aircraft was being evaluated by the Aeroplane and Armament Experimental Establishment.

In April 1935, in anticipation of a government contract, Hawker Siddeley started planning, jigging and tooling for a production run of 1,000 airframes. On 3 June a contract for 600 aircraft was received. These months saved in 1936 were later to provide the necessary time to build the several hundred extra machines so urgently needed for the Battle of Britain in 1940. Tooling was completed early in 1937 and on 12 October that year the first production Hurricane was flown.

Two months later the first RAF Hurricane Squadron, No. 111, received its aircraft at Northolt. By 1938 Hawker Siddeley was producing Hurricanes at the rate of one a day.

At the start of the war, on 3 September 1939, the Hawker Siddeley factories at Kingston, Brooklands and Langley, employed just over 4,000 people who were all engaged in the production of the Hurricane, 500 of which had already been delivered to the RAF. Production had also been undertaken at Hucclecote by the Gloster Aircraft Company and in Canada by the Canadian Car and Foundry Corporation.

By the time the Battle of Britain began, on 8 August 1940, 32 interceptor squadrons, out of the RAF's total of 52, were equipped with Hurricanes. They destroyed more enemy aircraft during this battle than the combined total of all other aircraft and anti-aircraft guns.

The success of this superb aircraft, in many roles throughout the world, has been well recorded. Nearly 15,000 Hurricanes were built. The final Hurricane, which is kept in immaculate condition, was purchased by Hawker Siddeley from the government in mid-1944. It is suitably inscribed "The Last of the Many". During the summer of 1968 it flew for the film *The Battle of Britain*.

Although maximum priority was given to the Hurricane production programme, other project work was going ahead. As early as 1936 both Rolls–Royce and Napiers were proposing 24

The upper photograph shows Snipes and Salamanders being built in the Sopwith factory in 1918. The lower one shows the same building 52 years later when Hawker Harriers were being built.

cylinder sleeve valve engines, developing almost twice the power of the Merlin.

In 1937 Hawker Siddeley commenced designing fighters for both these engines. The Tornado for the Rolls-Royce Vulture and the Typhoon for the Napier Sabre. The Tornado prototype was flown at the end of 1939, but because insufficient time had been allowed for the development of the Vulture engine, the Tornado did not go into squadron use. The Typhoon fared better. The prototype flew early in 1940. It proved to be very fast for its day. After lengthy development of the engine, weapon installations and airframe, the Typhoon won great favour as a ground attack aircraft, particularly when equipped with rocket projectiles, during the invasion of France in 1944.

Then in 1942 came the Tempest, a thin wing version of the Typhoon, with improved controls and powered for the most part by the Napier Sabre engine, although a number were fitted with the Bristol Centaurus engine. It possessed excellent low altitude characteristics. One Tempest Wing (roughly 60 aircraft) destroyed over 600 flying bombs aimed at the south of England in 1944.

The development of the Tempest led to the last of the Hawker Siddeley propeller-driven aircraft — the Fury, which was conceived in 1942. Backed by the Admiralty in 1943, the aircraft finally went into production in 1946 and was known as the Sea Fury. The Bristol Centaurus engine was, by then, fully developed and the aircraft gave good service to the Royal Navy, principally in the ground attack role in Korea. The Fury was also used by the Royal Australian, and Royal Canadian Navies and the Air Forces of Holland, Iraq, Egypt, Pakistan, Burma, Cuba, and in Western Germany for target towing.

Jet powered projects had been studied by Hawker Siddeley as early as 1941. Several design exercises were carried out by the company, but it was not until 1943, when preliminary details of a Rolls-Royce engine, later known as the Nene, were made available that the company began to harden on a design. Known initially as the P 1035 and later the P 1040, it was the first of a series of new airframes with the engine mounted amidships, behind the pilot.

Air intakes were in the leading edge of the wing roots and a split jet pipe (patented by Hawker Siddeley) was designed to exhaust the jet efflux from each side of the fuselage by the trailing edge of the wings. Initially supported by the Air Ministry, it was the Admiralty which eventually took the greater interest in this aircraft, a contract was received to build three prototypes to specification N 7/46 in 1946. Construction had already started as a private venture by this time.

Later, in 1946, following discussions with the Royal Aircraft Establishment, a research specification, E 38/46 was issued for the application of a swept wing to the P 1040 design, and a contract was received for the manufacture of two prototypes, which received the designation P 1052. The P 1040 flew from Farnborough for the first

The end of the line. The remarkable Hawker Harrier is now in service in a number of the world's air forces.

time in September 1947, and the P 1052 made its maiden flight in November 1948. At this time Hawker Siddeley production facilities were concentrated at Langley and Canbury Park Road, Kingston. Flight test facilities at Langley were fast becoming unsatisfactory due to restricted runways.

The test flying of the P 1040 and P 1052 was carried out from the RAE at Farnborough. London Airport, only 6 miles away, was growing rapidly and air traffic congestion was increasing. Clearly some other arrangements had to be made. The lease, held by Leyland Motors since 1928 on the more extensive factory premises on the Richmond Road, where Sopwith Aircraft were built 30 years previously, expired in 1948. Hawker Aircraft Limited took over the lease of the buildings and the experimental and production departments were moved there. The design department and machine shops remained in Canbury Park Road for a further 10 years. In 1950, Hawker Siddeley was fortunate to acquire the tenancy of Dunsfold airfield near Godalming. Langley was therefore vacated.

By this time one of the swept wing 1052 aircraft had been modified with all swept tail surfaces and a straight jet pipe, exhausting through the rear fuselage. This became the P 1081, in which the Australian Government showed interest. First flown in 1950, the P 1081 underwent extensive flight testing but the following year the aircraft was destroyed in an accident resulting in the death of its pilot, Sqd Ldr Wade. Meanwhile the P 1040 (to Specification N 7/46) had become the Sea Hawk for which the company received a production contract for 151 aircraft.

These were eventually made at Coventry by Armstrong Whitworth Aircraft Limited, and replaced the Sea Furies in the Royal Navy. Additional orders for the Sea Hawk were received from a number of countries.

In 1947 a new project design (Specification F 3/48) had been started as a private venture. This was the birth of the Hunter. A mock-up of the new aircraft was built in 1948. In the following year three prototypes were ordered and the first flew in 1951. Two years later the first production Hunter flew from Dunsfold. They also built a two-seater Hunter for pilot training which first flew in 1953. By 1960 almost 2,000 of these aircraft had been built.

As in the past, with one design completed, Sydney Camm at once turned his thoughts to its successor — the P 1083. It was a Hunter with a 50 degree swept wing and reheated Rolls-Royce Avon engine. It would have been the RAF's first supersonic fighter, had official attitudes not changed. The project was cancelled in favour of equipping the basic Hunter airframe with the Rolls-Royce 10,000 lb thrust series 200 Avon engine. This became the Hunter 6.

The full story of the Hunter's development and success throughout the world has been well recorded. It is fitting to note here that both Sir Thomas Sopwith and Sir Sydney Camm received their knighthoods for services to aviation in 1953, the year that the Hunter, flown by Neville Duke, established a new world speed record at 727.6 mph.

In 1957 the Government Defence White Paper forecast the end of manned fighter aircraft and so cancelled an order for 100 Hunters for the RAF. Hawker Siddeley recovered from this setback by selling Hunters in large numbers to India, Switzerland, Sweden, Rhodesia, The Netherlands, Belgium, Iraq, Lebanon, Jordan, Denmark and Peru and later to Saudi Arabia, Kuwait, Chile and Singapore.

Hunter development and production did not stop project work on a truly supersonic aircraft. In 1954 the design for a large, supersonic fighter, the P 1103, was submitted to the Air Ministry, but by 1956 the operational requirement shifted to lay emphasis on an aircraft capable of a dual role as an interceptor and tactical strike aircraft.

The P 1103 was extensively redesigned and construction as a private venture started. It was renamed the P 1121, and was to be capable of Mach 2.5. By 1958, much of the structure was complete but, by then, it had become clear that Hawker Siddeley would not be chosen to produce the aeroplane and so the company's project was cancelled. Parts of the airframe were presented later to the College of Aeronautics at Cranfield, where they can be seen today.

In 1957, while struggling to maintain Air Ministry interest in the P 1121, Hawker Siddeley received information from Bristol Engines about the BE 53 engine, an unusual twin spool design jet. The air from the front compressor could be directed downwards, or horizontally aft, through two rotatable nozzles, thus providing a form of vectored thrust. A study by the Hawker Siddeley project office led to the proposal of bifurcating the conventional jet pipe as in the Nene installation in the Sea Hawk and so exhausting the jet efflux through two rotatable nozzles similar in shape to those on each side of the plenum chamber aft of the front compressor. The four nozzles were arranged to rotate simultaneously and the total thrust from the engine could be directed downwards for vertical or hovering flight, or rearwards for conventional flight. The two front nozzles discharged cool air while the rear ones were subjected to the full heat of the total jet efflux.

A configuration embodying many original features, including the necessary jet reaction control system for use in hovering flight, was evolved and, by the end of 1957 the project had been given the number P 1127.

In 1958 funding for the engine was provided jointly by the United States Mutual Weapons Defense Program and Bristol Engines Limited. Hawker Siddeley again initiated progress by going ahead with the detailed design and manufacture of two prototype airframes.

The engine was first run on a test bed at Bristol in September 1959 and, in October 1960, the prototype P 1127 left the ground in hovering flight. By this time Hawker Siddeley had received contractual cover from the Government for the two prototypes and, in addition, four development airframes.

The Air Ministry watched this development with interest but, although an operational requirement was drafted around the concept, doubts were expressed about the usefulness of its subsonic performance. Although its development into a formidable new tactical aircraft was accurately forecasted the fact that it was not supersonic caused concern. It was felt, despite its potential for superior manoeuvrability, it would prove too slow against supersonic fighters.

In 1961 a NATO Military requirement, supported by the RAF, was published calling for a supersonic V/STOL (vertical or short take-off and landing) aircraft. This was met by a new Hawker Siddeley design, the P 1154, which was based on P 1127 principles but powered by the 33,000 lb vectored thrust BS 100 engine.

This far more advanced design nearly led to the demise of the P 1127 but fortunately, it was saved by a contract funded jointly by the United States of America, Federal Republic of Germany and Great Britain. This called for nine developed P 1127s, later called Kestrels, to evaluate close support V/STOL operations in the field, a programme which was admirably executed in the summer of 1965. Meanwhile, in 1963, the Government stated that, for reasons of economy, the P 1154 would be used by the Royal Navy in addition to the RAF. This resulted in a compromise aeroplane that neither service wanted. In 1964 the Royal Navy was permitted to break away from this doctrine and order the Phantom.

In January 1965 the P 1154 was cancelled by the Government, which, at the same time, issued a contract for the further development of the Kestrel and its Pegasus engine. The development aircraft was still known as the P 1127 and then, two years later, became the Hawker Siddeley Harrier. The RAF received their first single-seater (Mark 1) Harriers in 1969 and the two-seater (T.Mark 2) in 1970.

Sadly, on 12 March 1966, Sir Sydney Camm died at the age of 72. Tom Sopwith, his close associate for nearly 40 years, paid the following tribute to this outstanding engineer.

"Many people think that a design starts with a specification from the authorities, but with Camm this procedure was reversed. He considered that the uninterrupted experience he had in fighter design over a number of years enabled him to forecast the RAF's next requirement better than they could themselves. In other words he would produce a new design, incorporating various features which he knew the Air Ministry wanted, discuss it at length with the Air Ministry (and later the then Ministry of Supply) and in due course an official specification would be issued largely written around the tentative design he had originally submitted. This happened time and time again..."

Sir Thomas Sopwith ended his memorial address with the simple and very heartfelt words, "Thank you, Sydney".

The Harrier is still of great interest to many of the world's defence forces. It embodies the flexibility of the helicopter with the low level, high speed performance of the conventional jet fighter. Like the helicopter, its use is common to air force, navy, army and marine divisions of the Services.

The Hawker name continued to be used in the United Kingdom for a period of 55 years after Harry Hawker's untimely death in 1921. The company had a huge flair for anticipating aircraft trends. Technical advances were brought in at the right time, such as the sharp-nosed, low drag, liquid-cooled engines of the late 1920s and 1930s, the monoplanes of the 1940s, retractable undercarriages, swept wings and, most recently, vectored thrust.

But, above all, attention was paid to detailed design of mechanical parts and structures. Configurations were refined by intensive wind tunnel and flight development testing and last but not least, simplicity and not complexity was sought whenever possible.

A total of 37 types of aircraft bearing the Hawker name went into production. The names of all the aircraft which proudly bore the Hawker name are listed below although some of them were built in very small numbers.

Audax	Hoopoe
Cygnet	Hornbill
Danecock	Hornet
Danthorp	Horsley
Demon	Hotspur
Duiker	Hunter
Fury I	Hurricane
Fury II	Kestrel
Hardy	Nimrod
Harrier	Osprey
Hart	P.V.3.
Hartbeest	Sea Fury
Hawfinch	Sea Hawk
Hawk	Tempest
Hedgehog	Tomtit
Henley	Tornado
Heron	Typhoon
Hind	Woodcock

Epilogue

The History since WWII

It is now 100 years since Harry Hawker was born in Australia. During the last century, there have been dramatic developments in the aviation industry as a whole, as well as in the H.G. Hawker Engineering Company he helped to establish.

After Harry Hawker's death in 1921, Tom Sopwith led the Company through a period of phenomenal growth, merging with Armstrong Siddeley in 1935, and the de Havilland Aircraft Company in 1961. The Hawker Siddeley Group by then incorporated many of the famous names in British Aviation — Gloster, A.V. Roe, Blackburn, de Havilland, Folland, and many others.

In 1977, the British Government nationalized the UK aviation industry by forming British Aerospace. This incorporated the British Aircraft Corporation (BAC), and the two major aerospace operating subsidiaries of Hawker Siddeley Group — Hawker Siddeley Aviation (manufacturing civil and military aircraft), and Hawker Siddeley Dynamics (manufacturing missiles).

However, Hawker Siddeley Group retained an interest in aviation through their Australian and Canadian subsidiaries.

The Orenda Division of Hawker Siddeley Canada was involved in aircraft and engine manufacture for the Canadian Defence Forces, and is now a major gas turbine engine component manufacturer and repair and maintenance organization.

In Australia, the de Havilland Aircraft Company was formed in 1927, and became Hawker de Havilland Australia when the parent company in England merged with the Hawker Siddeley Group in 1961. The Australian Company manufactured Tiger Moths prior to the War, and went on to build Mosquitos, Vampires, and designed and built the Drover, a three-engined feederliner used for many years by the Royal Flying Doctor Service. More recently Hawker de Havilland Australia has successfully penetrated the international market, and has for many years been a sole source supplier to the major aircraft manufacturers of the world.

Major sub-assemblies manufactured by Hawker de Havilland are now in all Boeing 727, 737, 747, 757 aircraft; in the McDonnell Douglas MD80, and the Airbus A300, A310 and A320 models, and soon to be in

The Hawker Hawk. One of the last aircraft to bear the Hawker name. It is seen here flying over the Smalls in the Irish Sea, off St David's Head in Wales.

the A330/A340 aircraft. Components manufactured include wing ribs, elevators, doors, slats, and flaps for these aircraft.

In 1985, Hawker de Havilland purchased the Commonwealth Aircraft Corporation in Melbourne, and the Fisherman's Bend Plant is now manufacturing components for and assembling the General Electric T700 turboshaft engine for the Sikorsky Black Hawk and Sea Hawk helicopters, and the F404 engine for the F/A-18 Hornet fighter.

In Sydney, the Company manufactures and tests the Black Hawk helicopter as well as the PC9 turboprop Trainer.

Hawker de Havilland is now by far the largest aircraft manufacturer and aviation defence supplier in Australia, and has just announced a collaborative joint venture with the McDonnell Douglas Helicopter Company to design and manufacture the new MDX helicopter.

Hawker Pacific was formed in 1978 from the Sales and Aircraft Servicing Divisions of Hawker de Havilland. In the 11 years since its formation, this Company has expanded its aircraft servicing and spares distribution network throughout Australia and the Asian region, and has acquired a landing gear overhaul facility in Los Angeles, hydraulic overhaul facilities in Miami and Amsterdam, and a sales office in Bahrain. The Company represents and services a wide range of aviation products throughout Australia, Asia, Middle East, Europe and North America.

Aviation is once again a core business in Hawker Siddeley Group, and it is fitting that the Group's expertise is primarily based in Australia.

On Sunday 12 January 1989, the airport at Moorabbin in Victoria was officially renamed the Harry Hawker Airport. This is an especially notable recognition since, in recent times, airports have been named by their location rather than in honour of individuals. There is also a memorial building to Harry Hawker on the airport.

Bibliography

BOWYER, Chaz. *The History of the RAF*. Bison Books, 1977.

Britain's Glorious Navy. Odhams Press, 1944.

CHAMBERLAIN, Alan (Bob) Hawker. *The Chamberlain Story*.

CRAMPTON, John,   DFC, AFC and Bar, MRAeS. Paper read to the Institute of Mechanical Engineers at Kingston College of Technology, Kingston upon Thames, 28 November 1968.

      "   "   Lecture to the Royal Aeronautical Society. The Life & Work of H.G. Hawker AFC, 20 February 1979.

HAWKER, H.G. and Mackenzie Grieve K. *Our Atlantic Attempt*. Methuen & Co., 1919.

HAWKER, Muriel. *H.G. Hawker, Airman, His Life and Work*. Hutchinson & Co., London, 1922.

ROBERTSON, Bruce. *Sopwith — The Man and His Aircraft*. Autumn, 1970.

TUFFEN, Harold J., MBE, CEng, MRAeS and Tagg, Albert E., CEng, MRAeS. The Hawker Hurricane, Design Development and Production. Papers read to The Royal Aeronautical Society Historical Group, 18 November 1985.

WALLACE, Graham. *The Flight of Alcock & Brown, 14-15 June 1919*. Putnam, London, 1955.

Index